Matt Wolf

Sam Mendes at the Donmar
Stepping into Freedom

Foreword by Sam Mendes

Limelight Editions
New York

ACKNOWLEDGMENTS

   Theatres open their doors every night to the public but rarely does any theatre throw itself open to the degree of individual and archival access so graciously afforded by everyone at the Donmar Warehouse during the writing of this book. My thanks first off to Sam Mendes and Caro Newling for allowing me to be the Donmar's chronicler and for making themselves so fully and completely available during what was a characteristically busy few months for them both. The building's singular staff proved no less invaluable. Anne McNulty, Nick Frankfort, Julia Christie, Rachel Weinstein, and Dominic Fraser all gave generously of their time, and their memories, while Beth Key-Pugh, Tim Levy, and the tireless Sarah Hunt offered unceasing support and help that enabled the entire book to come together with terrifying speed. Tara Cook and Milly Leigh made clear that Donmar Films operates along the same cheerful and ever-cooperative lines as does the theatre office upstairs: a class act all round.

   Tracking down sixty-plus Donmar alumni for interviews wasn't always easy. My thanks to Susan d'Arcy for getting Colin Firth to a phone from the middle of a Buckinghamshire field ("the only place I can get reception") during a break in filming. Donna Coulling kept after Rachel Weisz until she rang one afternoon from a California motel. Ellie-Mae Aitken and Tracy Gossett made sure Nicole Kidman gave a call, and Jenny Turner did the same with Gwyneth Paltrow. Dena Hammerstein, Stuart Thompson, Richard Whitehouse, Lucinda Morrison, and Mary Parker kindly offered up necessary information or contacts - often both - and Clive Kaye saw me through the inevitable computer crises with his usual good cheer. Nick Hern's sharp and sensitive editing made any annotated "scribbles" (his word) a real pleasure to receive, while Elaine Steel and Clive Hirschhorn led me gently as well as scrupulously into the brave and intense world that is writing a book.

   My thanks, as always, go to my friends, who put up with what probably seemed a rather strange and sudden disappearing act. And to my parents, for taking me to the theatre to begin with, thereby first suggesting the matchless illumination that comes with a life spent in the dark.

Matt Wolf
September, 2002

contents

foreword

In an ideal world, theatres like the Donmar shouldn't have to exist. In an ideal world each major theatre in England could afford an ensemble, a lengthy rehearsal period, and possess an ongoing dialogue with a loyal audience. Over the years it would have developed an aesthetic, a methodology, and definable tastes. Something like this existed in the 1960s and 70s in England, when, looking across the theatre landscape one could see, amongst others, Gaskill and Dexter at the Royal Court, Olivier at the Old Vic, Hall and Nunn at the RSC, John Neville at the Nottingham Playhouse, Alan Dossor at the Liverpool Everyman, the beginnings of the Glasgow Citizens, and the Royal Exchange in Manchester. Definable aesthetics, beliefs in how theatre should be, disagreements, debate, opinion…

The 80s, of course, bought about the gradual erosion of this landscape, and with the glowing exception of Richard Eyre's regime at the National Theatre and one or two others, this erosion continues. It's a world now of freelance directors, all working in the same few theatres, all discussing the same few plays. A world where the desired theatre contract for a young actor or actress is a short one that can be fitted between television and film commitments, so, at the very least, he or she can pay their mortgage. It is a world of buckling under the weight of a new disease: celebrity obsession.

Is the Donmar a product of this, or in some small part a cause of it? I don't think that even I, having run the theatre for ten years, can objectively answer that question. But what I can say is that, despite all this, even because of it, something special happened in this small theatre in the middle of Covent Garden in the years 1992 to 2002, and this splendid book by Matt Wolf attempts in some way to celebrate and assess it.

When Caro Newling and I began our regime at the newly formed Donmar in 1992 we regularly brazened out questions about our immediate goals by answering that we believed in 'retrospective policy'. What we really meant was, "Wait three years and then we'll have worked out what our policy is". Well, luckily for us, a policy turned up. We followed our tastes, trusted our instincts, and tried to persuade the best directors and actors to come to us. Most of all, we ensured that pacing the foyers and brightly coloured stairways of the old banana warehouse were writers like Stephen Sondheim, Brian Friel, Athol Fugard, David Hare, Tom Stoppard, Harold Pinter, Alan Bennett, Michael Frayn, Peter Nichols, Kander and Ebb, Frank McGuinness, Joe Penhall, Paula Vogel, Richard Greenberg, David Mamet, David Auburn, and many others. So the new Donmar gradually emerged out of the mist: eclectic, entertaining, brazen, unapologetic in its pop-art aspirations and, consequently, mostly unfunded. How much of this was planned? Honestly? About two-thirds. The other third was a series of happy accidents. But then we were light on our feet, able to adapt, and, adhering to the 90s model, we could be a little more of a street fighter than theatres had traditionally been able, or needed to be.

by sam mendes

Occasionally, we played host not to plays, not even to theatre, but to cultural phenomena, and *The Blue Room* is dealt with at length in this book. It's true what Matt says about that period – it was a mixed blessing. But, make no bones about it, thereafter we were able to use its success and adapt at speed. We didn't cast another movie star until four years later when John Madden cast Gwyneth Paltrow in *Proof* (though there were no shortage of offers), but in that time, many people came to the theatre who had never come before, we trebled our Friends membership, and played to an average audience of 85%, whilst, most importantly, producing more new work than ever before.

Despite all this, I have a few regrets. I wish I'd pursued more relentlessly several new plays, including amongst others Terry Johnson's *Hysteria* and all of Kevin Elyot's (though in the end all these were done very well at the Royal Court). I wish I'd had more opportunities to promote some of our trainee directors to fully-fledged directors under our own roof. I wish we'd done more Shakespeare. I wish that, as wonderful as they are, we didn't need a whole department in our tiny theatre dedicated solely to fund-raising. In other words, I wish we'd had some money.

But one thing we did do well was plan for the future. Having had three terrific Associate Directors, one of them, Michael Grandage, is now taking over the theatre. I couldn't be more confident that he will make it his own, whilst understanding its particular and unique spirit.

Would I do it again somewhere else? Absolutely. Though it would probably again have to be from scratch. More satisfying, after all, to start a village shop than take over an existing franchise. On second thoughts, more of a junk shop, perhaps akin to David Mamet's creation in *American Buffalo*. There, as at the Donmar, things of true value and beauty simply pass through - Alan Cumming's beckoning finger in *Cabaret*, Stephen Dillane and his cricket bat in *The Real Thing*, Zoë Wanamaker and her single drop of blood in *Electra*, Nicole Kidman taking her first curtain call, Clive Rowe's joyous one-man show, the tank drill in the forest in *To the Green Fields Beyond*, the great John Kani twinkling in Fugard's *Playland*, Claire Skinner washing her glass figurines in *The Glass Menagerie*, Jim Broadbent's desperate, frantic dance of death at the end of *Habeas Corpus*, the kids singing that 'something is stirring' during *Merrily We Roll Along*, and on and on. No video shelf available for these, thank goodness. They live on in the building, in the memory, and now, in this book.

Sam Mendes
September, 2002

DONMAR

getting started

so what can you do
on a Saturday
night alone

chapter 1

"So what can you do on a Saturday night alone?" goes a lyric from one of the few Stephen Sondheim musicals (*Saturday Night*) that has not yet been produced at the Donmar Warehouse. In Sam Mendes' case, the answer was to decide to run a theatre.

It was October 28, 1989, and Mendes, then 24, was wandering through the West End, "sick with nerves," as he puts it, about the next day's reviews in the Sunday papers for his production of *The Cherry Orchard*. It scarcely mattered that six weeks later, the young director would have a second production - Boucicault's *London Assurance*, with Paul Eddington - up and running at the Haymarket. His focus for the moment was on a Chekhov play with Judi Dench and Bernard Hill in a new translation by Michael Frayn. "When you've got a play and a cast that good," Mendes recalls thinking, "who would get the blame if it went wrong?"

Still pondering the question, he turned off Neal Street, past the scaffolding and the boarded up warehouses of a significant swathe of Covent Garden that was primed for redevelopment. And there, affixed to the Earlham Street address that had for four important years (1977-1981) been the studio theatre of the Royal Shakespeare Company, was a sign saying, 'Closed Until Further Notice.' That seemed a rather final statement for a one-time hops brewery and then banana ripening warehouse that had first gone on to establish itself in arts circles as a rehearsal room for theatre and dance. The very name Donmar had its own honourable pedigree, dating to the 1950s and to the friendship at the time between the legendary London theatre manager, Donald Albery, and the dancer, Margot Fonteyn.

Mendes was intrigued as to the fate of so historic a building and asked his *Cherry Orchard* producer, Michael Codron, what was happening at this address. The answer was that it was a shell within a site that had been newly acquired by the local developers, Thomas Neal's. And as part of the conditions laid down by Camden Council to rebuild the entire block, this particular space had to be preserved as a theatre. What kind of theatre? No one knew.

Before long, Mendes was sitting in the office of George Biggs, then the number two to Roger Wingate, whose Chesterfield Properties had in 1989 taken over Maybox Theatres, one of which was the defunct Donmar studio space. "I strode in and said to George, 'I can run that theatre.' Jesus Christ," says Mendes, not completing his sentence. "If I had known what was up ahead..."

Biggs quickly introduced Mendes to Wingate, who was pleased, he says, to have an answer "to a question that I hadn't even put." Since that time, Wingate has moved on to chair ACT Productions, the

> **Sam was amazing: from the second he brought me in to have a conversation, he made it very clear that he wanted me to have a relationship with the building: the Donmar family grabbed me and hauled me in and attached me.**
>
> **I think it took me a long time to figure out that the bigger the piece, the better the Donmar space would respond. It can be quite an unforgiving space on the designer - it's about ten feet too shallow and you can't fix an image, which makes it very hard. And the upstage left corner is a bit of a killer; you can't do much with it.**
>
> **I suppose when I came to the Donmar, it seemed to me to be a very sexy new space or maybe a very sexy reinvention of an old space by somebody who, rather interestingly, could have let his career go a very, very different path. And the rest of Sam's career hasn't suffered in any way; he hasn't denied himself anything to work at the Donmar. I think Sam is the fastest learner of any human being I have ever met; he has an ability to synthesise how you actually perform a task pretty stunningly.**

JOHN CROWLEY, director
The Maids, 1997
How I Learned To Drive, 1998
Into the Woods, 1998
Juno and the Paycock, 1999
Tales From Hollywood, 2001

producing entity whose London and/or Broadway credits include the revivals of Noises Off and The Elephant Man and Charlotte Jones's award-winning play, Humble Boy. But at the end of the 1980s he had found himself in charge of a theatre whose future was by no means clear. Maybe the Donmar - properly rebuilt - could be a central London version of the Hampstead Theatre, whose former artistic director, Michael Attenborough, had come in to advise Wingate as to a possible way forward. If nothing else, the potential existed for a proscenium-arched equivalent to the Hampstead in the middle of town.

One day, says Wingate, "Sam came to see me and told me I had got it all wrong: the whole charm of the building was the configuration as it had been" - i.e. on three sides, with very little distance between the performers and their public. "If I kept that," Wingate was told, "Sam thought that all sorts of people would be interested in working there because of the relationship of the space to the audience." Wingate's reaction? "I thought it made sense; Sam had obviously thought through what he was saying. I phoned him up and said that if he ran the theatre for us, I would take his advice."

The offer appealed to Mendes, who - though that little bit too young to have known the Warehouse (as it was then called) in its RSC days - had seen numerous productions during the subsequent period when it was a receiving house programmed by Nica Burns. Since 1993, Burns has worked as a Production Director for the Really Useful Theatre group, Andrew Lloyd Webber's company. But from January 1984, she was for almost six years responsible for booking work into the Donmar, touring shows mostly: Druid Theatre from Ireland, Deborah Warner's Kick Theatre, Declan Donnellan's Cheek By Jowl, and so on. "It was exciting, cutting edge, risky work," says Burns, who went on take a great interest in Mendes' regime as a board member for nine out of the ten years of his Donmar directorship. The theatre's aim under her guidance, she says, had been "not to do anything in a conventional way."

That ethos didn't have to be expressly stated to appeal to Mendes, who had no sooner arrived at Peterhouse, Cambridge (the former home to Mendes' friend and colleague Richard Eyre) before he was

Architects Renton Howard Wood Levin planned several incarnations for the Donmar before building work could begin and the new Donmar could open its doors directing the David Halliwell play, *Little Malcolm and His Struggle Against the Eunuchs*. Mendes had grown up in London and then in Oxford, where he and the theatre designer Tom Piper were in the same year at Magdalen College School. (Later, Piper worked as Mendes' designer at the National Theatre on

a revival of *The Birthday Party*; the professional reunion of the two schoolmates, says Mendes, was "very moving.") Mendes opted for Cambridge in part, he says, "because I knew Oxford so well" and arrived on campus intending to study art history. Some early thought had even been given to a career as a journalist.

What about theatre? "I didn't know that was a job, in a way," he explains. "Drama was acting; the rest just didn't occur to me, I suppose." It took time (and a shift to a degree in English, where he wrote two separate theses) before Mendes saw the potential appeal of directing. It helped, of course, that he had seen Beckett's *Waiting For Godot* and *Endgame* at Oxford Playhouse, not to mention numerous student productions of Shakespeare, including a version of *A Midsummer Night's Dream* early on at school with the future director Katie Mitchell and the actor Tom Hollander among the cast. (Both would end up working at various times at Mendes' Donmar.) Having wanted to write, Mendes soon saw the appeal of directing: "Here was this discipline that united all the things that I loved: it had a literary bent, but there was also something about creating an alternative universe and then populating and controlling it."

And direct Mendes did, staging Berkoff's *East*, the bloody Jacobean drama *The Changeling* ("I did that terribly; God, it was a disaster") and a one-man version of Gogol's *Diary Of A Madman*, among others. His campus production of *Endgame* travelled north to Edinburgh. Mendes' taste, he says, was still pretty much unformed: "I hadn't found my style, and I was mimicking people - copying what I thought was good theatre. I didn't have a

> 66 **The Donmar has always been a very supportive place to work, and interestingly enough, a lot of the same people are still there ten years later. In this business, that's extremely unusual. What's weird about the space is it's very tall: you notice this as a lighting designer, of course - it's intimate by virtue of its proximity to the audience and yet also quite epic; that back wall goes up a long way. That wall is great; I love it. It always looks sexy. There's something about knowing you're in a found space that's not trying to be neutral. You can put anything in front of it, and it always looks good. It's a space that encourages the imagination of the audience, which, of course, is the best possible thing. You don't need to show reality; you just need to suggest it. Now I live around the corner from the theatre, I'm trying to tell them they should only employ locals.** 99

RICK FISHER, lighting designer
The Life of Stuff, 1993
The Threepenny Opera, 1994
The Maids, 1997
Boston Marriage, 2001
Lobby Hero, 2002

voice at all, and I didn't have an aesthetic." At that point, being a theatre director, Mendes thought, meant presenting a certain image - the leather jacket, the fags, the "down and dirty" persona: all the qualities, indeed, that a particular student director called Tim Supple, who was in the year ahead, possessed in spades. (Supple went on to pursue his own professional directing career at the Young Vic and the RSC, among other addresses.) Before he knew it, Mendes had graduated and sent off fifty or so letters to various theatres, pretty sure instead that he would end up doing something in TV.

It was during finals week that Mendes heard from John Gale, who was writing from the Chichester Festival Theatre to invite the imminent graduate to come for a visit. Not that Chichester, with its decidedly starry past, meant much at the time to Mendes, who knew about the Royal Court and the National and the Oxford Playhouse but nothing, he says, "about the home counties." Nor was Mendes particularly persuaded upon arrival by the hexagonal placards in the car park advertising a season made up of *Hay Fever*, *A Man For All Seasons*, and *Miranda* (an adaptation of Goldoni's *Mirandolina*), starring Penelope Keith. "I thought, 'I'm in the wrong place; this is ridiculous,'" says Mendes. But a love of cricket shared with John Gale put a different spin on things and Mendes was hired, his starting salary £42 a week: "I was a charming young man, but cricket, frankly, sealed the deal." Signed

Prior to taking over the Donmar, Sam Mendes was busy directing elsewhere. His *Troilus and Cressida* for the Royal Shakespeare Company starred Amanda Root and Ralph Fiennes▼ and introduced him to the RSC employee who later became his Donmar number two, Caro Newling. His National Theatre credits include ▼Alison Steadman and Jane Horrocks in *The Rise and Fall of Little Voice* and Judi Dench in *The Sea* ▲

for one year as an associate director, Mendes saw himself as a glorified gofer, mopping the stage in the Chichester tent that was their studio theatre then. He was working alongside someone called Toby Stephens, whom Mendes remembers as a "spotty, incredibly shy child with a big quiff ; he was incredibly sweet." (Stephens' parents, Robert Stephens and Maggie Smith, had been part of Chichester during its heyday under Laurence Olivier. It was the youth's stepfather, Beverley Cross, who had written the adaptation of *Mirandolina*.)

By the end of September, 1987, Mendes had made his professional directing debut: a one-off evening of two Chekhov plays, *The Bear* and *The Proposal*. Looking back, Mendes describes the double bill as "Brecht meets Chekhov," typifying the taste of a wannabe maverick who, he says by way of self-assessment, was "well into the B's": Brecht, Barker, Bond. How were the plays? "I don't think Chekhov has ever been so maltreated. We had lots of funny walks and Sinatra playing; it was very Pythonesque." What mattered was that John Gale liked the evening enough to offer Mendes a job running the Chichester studio space. That position in turn left Mendes well placed to take on the directorship of the theatre's purpose-built Minerva auditorium in its inaugural season the following year. In between summer assignments down in Sussex, Mendes had got work at the Arts Theatre, Cambridge, directing *Cyrano de Bergerac* for the Marlowe Society, with Tom Hollander as Cyrano. That was followed early in 1989 by a Tim Firth play, *Cardboard City*, at the Soho Poly in London. But it was his opening Minerva production in 1989 of the sweeping Russian drama *Summerfolk* - with a cast including Lesley Sharp, Dearbhla Molloy, and again Tom Hollander - that began to establish Mendes in a serious way. Says Mendes: "What the theatre wanted, really, was [Noël Coward]'s *Cavalcade* or something similarly celebratory and festive,

▲ The newly renovated Donmar unveils its first design: Anthony Ward's shooting gallery set for *Assassins*

and here I was doing a Botho Strauss version of Gorky which, frankly, was quite daring."

The audacity worked. Within weeks, Mendes had been tapped to assume the reins on a production of *London Assurance*, following the departure after two days of its director, Robin Phillips, who had suffered what Mendes calls a "massive crisis of confidence." The same wasn't likely to befall the young Mendes whom an early colleague, the distinguished arts executive Genista McIntosh, would quickly recognise as "preternaturally confident." John Gale ordered Mendes to take over Phillips' production, and so he did. "I'd only heard the readthrough," says Mendes. "I hadn't read *London Assurance*; I didn't know anything about it." Six months later, the Boucicault comedy was following *The Cherry Orchard* into the West End.

The offers soon came thick and fast: Judi Dench rang her friend Dearbhla Molloy for a report on Mendes. Spoken of approvingly to the satisfaction of his star, he was signed to direct the production of *The Cherry Orchard* with designs by Paul Farnsworth, who had done *Summerfolk*. (In 1991, Mendes directed both Dench and Molloy in a Young Vic production of *The Plough and the Stars*.) At the end of 1989, Genista McIntosh and Terry Hands made available a slot at the RSC. Mendes filled it with a *Troilus and Cressida* featuring one of the defining actors of Mendes' career, Simon Russell Beale, as a mightily pestilential Thersites. At the same time, there was no mistaking Mendes' frequent return as an audience member to the various shows that the Donmar Warehouse had been presenting in town. "It really felt like home to the sort of work I wanted to be doing," Mendes says of the theatre under Nica Burns, "even though it wasn't a producing house. It was a vibe thing - where it is, the shape of the auditorium, the atmosphere when you walk in. It felt happening, and it still does."

And so it happened that Mendes wanted the Donmar and that Roger Wingate and George Biggs

Louise Gold and Cathryn Bradshaw in *Assassins* ▲

wanted him. In the young applicant's favour, says Wingate, was someone "who wasn't trying to make an impression; he just spoke common sense. Sam was clearly very intelligent and just very likable, and that was a very important factor. He was somebody of whom you felt, 'I could trust him.'" George Biggs thought the Donmar needed a firmer identity than it could have as a receiving house, in order, he says, "to make the place more exciting." Mendes, then, was the right person at the right time. Adds Biggs: "Certainly, I wouldn't have been able to programme that building as a producing venue because I would not have had the experience. One needed an artistic director to choose the product and have the theatre be his little baby and get on with it."

"Sam took me and the project in a direction," says Roger Wingate, "that I hadn't had in mind" - which meant hiring not just Mendes ("Sam said to me, 'Would I get a salary?'" Wingate recalls) but a support staff. At which point, enter executive producer Caro Newling, the person behind the theatre's decade-long rise and rise. "Caro came on board," says Wingate, who was able to better her RSC salary by some £2000, "and that was the big turning point, obviously." And so was born a crucial partnership in the British theatre of the 1990s.

Nine years Mendes' senior, Newling was no less steeped in theatre, having got a job at Theatre Royal, Stratford East, within two weeks of leaving Warwick University in 1978. At Warwick, where she read French and Theatre Studies, Newling had been a contemporary of the actor Alex Jennings and the producers Lucy Neal and Rose de Wend Fenton, who between them founded the London International Festival of Theatre (LIFT). At Stratford East, says Newling, "they took me on because I had a lisp so when I was nervous, they would know I was bullshitting them." Newling spent two-and-a-half years at that

venue, working first for Clare Venables and then during the last six months for Philip Hedley, before moving on to various jobs at the Royal Opera House, Ballet Rambert, the Almeida. Then came the move to a nearly seven-year stint at the Royal Shakespeare Company, where Newling ended up head of press. And it was there on level seven of the Barbican, back when Mendes was directing *Troilus*, that he and Newling first met. "You would look up," Newling remembers, "and there Sam would be quietly scanning the papers, reading everything. He knew that the press office - which wasn't the trendiest place to be - was where you picked up all the information. Sam was always interested in what was being said and how it was handled." Mendes likes to say that the two owed their friendship to the fact that Newling's desk faced the door - so she was the first to see him every time he entered the room.

Newling had been at the RSC during the debacle in the late 1980s over *Carrie*, the musical, directed by Terry Hands, that became a lightning rod for controversy. (Intriguingly, that show's star, Barbara Cook, owed the renaissance of her career in Britain to a 1987 cabaret season at the Donmar in its previous

▲ Caro Newling, the Donmar's executive producer and Sam Mendes' number two

DONMAR WAREHOUSE

AT THOMAS NEAL'S

Play it again, Sam: how Sam Mendes resurrected the Donmar Warehouse

GEORGE BIGGS, the middle-aged theatrical impresario in the wide-striped suit with the bloodhound eyes, is a tolerant man. As head of Maybox, the theatre management company, his heart may lie with the red velvet foyers and the Dutch choc mint chip of the West End scene – he runs Wyndhams, the Comedy, the Albery. But a glance at the banners above these theatres reveals a smattering of new writing nesting comfortably between the Lloyd Webbers and the farces. It is George Biggs, you're reminded, who holds the lease to the Donmar Warehouse. He's the man who did the deal with Sam.

Sam Mendes, the young theatre director with the darting eyebrows, is an ambitious man. He was around the Donmar back in early 1990, after it had just been closed down. He saw the dust-sheets, the scaffolding, and he knew what he wanted. 'I wanted that theatre. I liked where it was – the middle of town. I liked the way it looked. I was excited at the thought of running an experimental stage in a West End setting. And most of all the chance to open my own theatre rather than take one over from someone else.'

Mendes approached Biggs, who was...

'I'm tire...

In good company: Sam Mendes (centre) with colleagues (clockwise from left) Richard Hull, Nick Frankfort, Paul Williams, Caro Newling, George Biggs, Dominic Fraser and Anne McNulty.

PHOTOGRAPH BY JILLIAN EDELSTEIN

THE INDEPENDENT Saturday 25 July 1992

CUL**TURE** / Later this year, the director Sam Mendes will open the Donmar Warehouse to playgoers after some 15 months of preparation. Thomas Sutcliffe reports on the long road to running your own theatre

Theatre in twenty stages

GERAINT LEWIS

Gary Parker, site manager, Sam Mendes, artistic director, and Caro Newling, administrative director, in the interior of the Donmar Warehouse

...A THEATRE

...nd you. As Sam Mendes ...rs it, the path towards ...his own theatre started on ...to another. "When I was ...e *Cherry Orchard* in ...nd I passed the Donmar ...ust ripped down the doors ...re were lots of old posters ...around. I asked Michael ...n [the theatrical impre-... 'What's going to happen to ...onmar?' He told me they ...going to refurbish it and gave ... contact."

MAKE THE CALL

...ng George Biggs, who runs ...box [the West End theatre ...agers], and said 'Look, I've ...his wonderful idea. Why don't ...treat this just like another the-...e, but allow me to run a pro-...tion company? To my great ...prise he says yes."

Mendes's doubt is understand-...le; his career, while not quite in ... infancy still doesn't have to ...have very often. But a quick look ...his reviews no doubt helped ...iggs make up his mind. Critical ...and commercial success both at ...he RSC and in the West End pre-...sumably quietened a business-...man's anxiety about handing over ...a theatre which would have to ...combine elements of both. And ...the prospect of having a source of ...high-quality productions which ...might transfer into other Maybox ...theatres won't have done any ...harm.

3 □ BURN YOUR BOATS

"I signed the contract and put it in ...the post on Boxing Day [1991]; it ...was like posting in three years of ...my life. I'd never signed myself ...away for such a long period of ...time."

4 □ FIND AN ARCHITECT

Mendes and Newling didn't have ...to look far; as the Donmar is being ...refurbished as part of a larger ...commercial development, archi-...tects were already in place. But ...they arrived in the nick of time. ..."There had been other people in-...volved who suggested that the the-...atre be turned round to form a ...small proscenium stage," recalls ...Mendes. "So when I turned up for ...my first meeting with the architect ...[Gordon Forbes], I was presented ...with a model of a theatre which ...was completely unlike the one I ...had remembered. I threw up my ...

9 □ DRAW UP CONTRACTS

"We had to start with the unions," says Newling. ..."but it's very easy for them to see, when you look ...

...ment then, the house-style is flowing from the ...West ...

11 □ ARRANGE YOUR SEATING

"We wanted to get 268 because it would increase ...amount of revenue," says Newling, but in fact ...they've had to settle for 252 because of safety re-...quirements, a change which resulted in a recal-...standard of ...al budgets. "We've elected to use ...

...bles at the bait of a West End ...presence for a Fringe expenditure. ...They need £200,000 to cover four ...productions a year and are build-...ing their appeal to private donors ...on the guarantee that money will ...flow into creative costs – props ...will benefit from donations of £25 ...plus, for example, while those over ...£100 will go to costumes.

14 □ FIX YOUR SEASON

"I'm hoping that at least 50 per ...cent of the season will be made up ...of new work," says Mendes. "*As-...sassins*, as far as I'm concerned, is ...a new work, because it's the Eng-...lish premiere of a piece by ...Sondheim. Stephen sent it to us ...on the advice of Richard Eyre at ...the National . . . I took it straight ...away as a fascinating piece which ...fitted perfectly into the space. It ...was actually going to be the third ...show but our dates were put back ...and I thought 'what the hell, it's an ...event'. We would now feel odd ...considering anything else to open ...with, it feels so natural."

15 □ START A CASTING LIBRARY

"We did write around to agents ...who had the sort of client list we ...wanted to see for *Assassins*," says ...Newling. "And, once you start to ...see people, word gets around to ...other agencies and then after that ...individuals start to send in their ...CVs, so you build up a casting li-...brary. Agents were ringing on a ...daily basis expecting to talk to a ...casting department. Well, that ...was whoever was on the phone, ...usually me."

16 □ ARRANGE THE INSURANCE

"Maybox is looking after building ...and personnel," explains Newling. ..."We will insure individual produc-...tions as we go along. We didn't ...want an understudy system – be-...cause our standard salaries are ...fairly low anyway we felt it would ...be wrong to pay some people ...more for understudy obligations. ...So we looked into insuring against ...losing a production and realised in ...the end that it was more cost-ef-...fective to carry the understudy ...payments."

17 □ MEET THE NEIGHBOURS

"We went to see the Covent Gar-...den Community Association, be-...cause there'd been concern from ...residents about our application ...for a license for late-night perfor-...mances," says Newling. "We came ...to an agreement in the end that ...we could programme late-night activities up to ...1.30am on Friday and Saturday and that there ...would be 12 weeks of the year when we could pro-...gramme up to 1.00am on weekdays.

18 □ APPLY FOR CHARITABLE STATUS

This is essential for most arts organisations. The ...National and the RSC both have charitable sta-...made easier in the case of th...

▲ Casting director Anne McNulty

regime.) And it was Newling who was on the front line against the campaign that was then being waged by various newspapers to discredit the workings of subsidised theatre, many of them boasting so-called "Insight Teams" (or the equivalent) "making accusations that," Newling says, "were wrong." It was hardly a surprise, then, that she leapt at the chance when Genista McIntosh brokered a meeting between Mendes and Newling. Over coffee on the Barbican terrace, Mendes broached the topic of taking on an all-new Donmar. Says Newling: "I said 'yes' before Sam had even finished the sentence."

At first, the aim was to open the building in 1991, an ambitious scheme that failed to account for the inevitable complexity of building works and planning, not least when it comes to theatres. Mendes was able to go off and direct elsewhere, which left Newling on her own for seven months up under the roof of the Albery, a dead pigeon seemingly ensconced for keeps on the windowsill. "I got very very depressed and incredibly lonely; I found it incredibly hard." Respite came first via Olivia Wingate, Roger's daughter, who was brought in for the summer holidays, and, more far reachingly, via a former Young Vic employee, Anne McNulty, a warm and welcoming Mancunian who quickly became an essential player in the Donmar team. Says Mendes: "I

▲ The TVs encircling the set for Phyllida Lloyd's semi-futuristic production of *The Threepenny Opera*

said to Anne, 'Basically, everything Caro and I can't do, you've got to do.'" Taken on as an all purpose production administrator, McNulty neatly segued to casting, where her innate sunniness helped allay the anxieties that often besiege the casting process. So delicate and specific is the job that ten years and several administrative premises on, McNulty is the only Donmar employee with her own office. In casting, of course, privacy is key.

Donmar technical and production manager Dominic Fraser ▲

While the Albery Theatre downstairs was hosting Sandi Toksvig in *The Pocket Dream* and Pauline Collins and then Patricia Hodge in *Shades*, Newling and McNulty saw their staff expand. The chosen production manager was Dominic Fraser, who had spent three years as the Albery's master carpenter only to move over to the Donmar following a promise from George Biggs that the new job wouldn't be too tough. "I was told there wouldn't be any scenery," says Fraser, "that each show would just be a couple of armchairs and a table." Instead, he ended up overseeing in the years to come the construction and installation of more than seventy-five sets of considerable degrees of complexity: not bad for an auditorium with very little depth, scant wing space to the right of the stage and none at all on the left. It was Fraser who had first to find and then to look after the televisions - nearly fifty in all - that were placed around the set for Phyllida Lloyd's semi-futuristic production of *The Threepenny Opera*. Or monitor the often vertigo-defying staircases that became something of a Donmar constant, from *Design For Living* through *Company* to *The Little Foxes*. Or even warn Tom Stoppard against excitedly making a point while walking on a newly varnished stage lest (this almost happened) he got stuck.

A second Albery employee, Nick Frankfort, was tapped to be the Donmar's company stage manager. (After some time away, Frankfort later graduated to general manager, the post directly below Newling.) His early work at the Donmar brought challenges that were certainly new. At the Albery, Frankfort was accustomed to wearing a suit while opening champagne for Patricia Hodge's guests. Such formality was inconceivable at the Donmar, where Frankfort was soon engaged lugging crates for *Assassins*. Or having a plaster of Paris cast made of his toe and then filled with black syrup to use as a prop for the macabre comedy, *The Life of Stuff*. Frankfort's gift for swift thinking proved central to one of his later incarnations at the Donmar: the programmer of what became an invaluable annual summer season of London cabaret known as *Divas at the Donmar*, Frankfort during

Donmar general manager Nick Frankfort joins Sam Mendes at the theatre's 10th-anniversary party, held in the Sussex countryside July 28, 2002 ▲

that time looked after such performers as Patti LuPone, Betty Buckley, Siân Phillips, Michael Ball, Imelda Staunton and, indeed, Barbara Cook. (Clive Rowe has been a male "diva" twice.) And yet, how many of them required the quick-changes with which Frankfort was one night confronted in 1993 when Alan Cumming's dresser on *Cabaret* arrived late, leaving Frankfort to do the job?

> **"Even before I did a play there, the Donmar was already to me the kind of place that had made theatre sort of an event: *Cabaret* had been on and had been not just a play but a phenomenon. So to me it was the place that seemed to make theatre very funky and cool. It was serious - there was new writing and there were classics being done again and there was always a real excitement around the work.**
>
> **It is an incredibly intimate space, and you're very exposed; you have to be very truthful because people otherwise will notice. The audience is sitting right there next to you, as if they were having coffee across a table.**
>
> **I always hallucinate my dad is in the audience; I always go, 'God, dad was in tonight,' and it's never him; he's already been twice.**
>
> **It's the kind of place where I feel I could go and visit the office any day and just say 'hi,' which is a really lovely feeling. As an actor, you move through so many spaces that you don't have a permanent workplace. At the Donmar, they make you feel like you belong there - and they do that to everyone who works there. "**

RACHEL WEISZ, actress
Design For Living, 1994
Suddenly Last Summer (Warehouse Productions), 1999

The personnel in place, Mendes and Newling in September, 1992, moved their team to offices in the same building as the Donmar, which was preparing to open its doors the following month. (It was during the Four Corners New Writing season in 1997 that they moved offices again - this time to a far bigger administrative home just round the corner at their present Neal Street address.) An opening show, meanwhile, had been agreed - Stephen Sondheim's *Assassins*, Mendes' original idea of *The Front Page* having been delayed on the grounds that it was too costly at the time. (The classic American comedy was ultimately produced at the Donmar in the Christmas slot in 1997.) *Assassins* had come via Richard Eyre at the National Theatre, who passed the show on to Mendes. "I heard the CD and thought, 'Oh, I get it completely,'" recalls Mendes. "*Assassins* seemed a wildly eccentric project, but it was a Sondheim premiere, and a true original."

It had taken £1.3 million in building works alone to get the Donmar ready for London, not to mention all manner of byzantine negotiations backstage to persuade the developer to allow the Donmar a rent-free deal for the first five years. In addition, launched without a penny of public funding, the theatre would have to be self-financing (impossible) or hugely sponsored (difficult, though Carlton was on board with a three-year deal by January, 1993). While the artistic team was plotting a first season, Wingate and Biggs were planning an experiment in unsung subsidy, whereby they would underwrite the Donmar's output for Mendes' first three years. After that, it was sink or swim.

At the time, however, the concerns of the creative team were more immediate: Raising the stage and sinking the stalls; finding the audience for a nine-week run of an unknown Stephen Sondheim musical; spreading the word via publicists Lynne Kirwin and Mary Parker that here was a hip, young team of theatre-makers. In PR terms, youth was absolutely key, says Kirwin. "There weren't any interviews or statements about policy." There was time enough (1996, to be precise) for the Donmar to become a completely independent registered charity, Donmar Warehouse Projects, while it would take the theatre seven years to become a revenue-funded client of the Arts Council. But none of that mattered nearly as much as the artistic possibilities of a playhouse that seemed capable of taking on all forms of performance, from a one-woman show to a big musical, a centuries-old play to a modern classic. The Donmar could rock one minute - Ruby Turner's "diva" season in August, 2002, all but blew the theatre roof off - and feel uniquely forensic and intimate the next.

That sense of possibility was the appeal of a space that would find five of the Donmar's original staff still working there a decade later. "It's incredibly inviting," says Caro Newling, "like stepping into freedom."

As well as being an early Sam Mendes production, the Marlowe Society *Cyrano* of 1988 contained several other luminaries:

Allie Burns (actress)

Edmund Butler
(World Service presenter)

Jonathan Cake (actor)

Nick Clegg (Euro MP)

Will Eaves (journalist)

Pippa Harris
(Head of drama
commissioning BBC)

Tom Hollander (actor)

Ian Kelly (actor)

Tim Lusher (journalist)

Vicky Mortimer (designer
- now Vicki Mortimer)

Henry Naylor
(actor/comedian 'Boff' in
Barclaycard adverts)

Tom Piper (designer)

Brian Skeet (filmmaker)

John Walters (actor
- now Jack Waters -
married to Emily Watson)

CAMBRIDGE UNIVERSITY MARLOWE SOCI

THE 1988 PRODUCTION OF CYRANO DE BERGERAC AT THE ARTS THEATRE CAMBR

PRODUCTION TEAM

Director	Sam Mendes.......65 Great Eastern Street	
Producer	Pippa Harris......3 Victoria Street	242157
Set Designer	Tom Piper........94 Thoday Street	323217
		244093
Assistant Director	Brian Skeet.......6 Adams Road	
Assistant Producer	Tim Lusher........Clare College	
Publicity Designer	Clare Harris.....Robinson College	316021
Stage Manager	Paola Grenier....40 Grange Road	333200
A.S.M	Raphaelle Sadler	311431
Costume Designer	Vicky Mortimer	357294
Costume Assistants	Tamsin Harris,Catherine Taylor	
Musical Director	Corin Buckeridge	
Fight Director	Caroline Backhouse	
Publicity	Dan Merzov	
Props	Jenny Wilson, Jo Howard	
Make Up	Bella King	

CAST

Charlie Burkitt	Nick Clegg		
Allie Burns	Will Eaves	Jon Harris	Nick Papadopoulos
Richard Bushell	Kate Eden	Mary Harvey	Charles Prideaux
Edmund Butler	John Edmondson	Tom Hollander	Katy Walters
John Cake	Ros Furlong	Ian Kelly	John Walters
		Henry Naylor	Tanya White

something is stirring

stephen sondheim
at the donmar

chapter 2

"I do think the shows I've been associated with are closely related to plays," says Stephen Sondheim. So it makes sense, after all, that a defining musical talent was the person to emerge over the Mendes decade as the Donmar's de facto house dramatist.

The theatre on four occasions in nine years has reached into the Sondheim repertoire. *Assassins* was a European premiere, while *Company* and *Into the Woods* were studio theatre revivals of big and successful Broadway shows. *Merrily We Roll Along* was known in London from concert performances and a Guildhall student production but had never previously sustained a local run. And nowhere to date has a show that did a shockingly fast fade on Broadway in 1981 been so sufficiently revalued that it could re-emerge two decades later in time to win the 2001 Olivier Award as the season's best "new" musical.

Sam Mendes sees a logic to Sondheim's repeated success at the Donmar: "He's just brilliantly suited to the space. For one thing, Steve has a wonderful enthusiasm about ways of producing his work, and that's why so many productions of his shows are available to a director - because he encourages different voices. There's a kaleidoscopic range of possibilities that his shows allow. I've always seen them as music theatre rather than musicals. They have a poetry, an emotional resonance, that really override any conventional theatrical framework."

And if that was to be the case, the composer was more than happy to comply. A dedicated Anglophile since his first visit to Britain in 1952, Sondheim first worked professionally in London in 1958, when *West Side Story* had its West End premiere at Her Majesty's. Since then he has seen his work spawn two widely travelled theatre revues (*Side By Side By Sondheim* and *Putting It Together*), both of which began in England, where in 1990 he was the inaugural Cameron Mackintosh Visiting Professor of Contemporary Theatre at St. Catherine's College, Oxford. By the time, therefore, that *Assassins* had been selected to inaugurate the new Donmar, Sondheim knew, so to speak, the score. "The notion of this kind of high-class Off-Broadway theatre for *Assassins* seemed exactly right: Sam clearly knew what the piece was about, and had a real enthusiasm for it."

The question was what enthusiasm Britain might have for a typically audacious Sondheim venture that had already to that point had a rather peculiar New York history. This creator's subject matter, of course, is rarely orthodox. Who else would think in *Sunday In the Park With George* of writing a score that mirrored in musical terms the pointillism of a French Impressionist painter? Or elevate a potential penny-dreadful like *Sweeney Todd* to a musical that is nearly Benjamin Britten-esque in its breadth? But

◀ Adrian Lester

> **❝** There's not much you can do with the Donmar as a space, so in that respect whatever the show is, is really dependent on the writing, the directing, the performing. In the end, you're quite naked out there; people can almost see your thoughts.
>
> Sam's concentration is quite phenomenal. Even if he's getting tired, his focus is still 100%, and also his sense of fun. Anne is a gorgeous woman, and Caro, too. **❞**

CIARAN HINDS, actor

Assassins, 1992
Richard III, 1993

even by Sondheim's standards, audiences Off-Broadway may have been unprepared for the premiere early in 1991 of a musical about the rogues' gallery of those who, at various times throughout the nation's fractious history, had attempted to assassinate the President of the United States.

Sondheim had written about real people before - Georges Seurat, for instance, in *Sunday In the Park*. But the anxieties besetting a fiercely self-absorbed painter were bound to be less troubling to audiences than the worrisome psychic landscape exposed by the line-up of obsessive social deviants that *Assassins*, revue-like, put on parade. Some - John Hinckley and Lynette (Squeaky) Fromme - were better known than others, just as the assassins' various targets varied in terms of recognition, too (from Abraham Lincoln and Ronald Reagan to James Garfield and William McKinley).

Even in America, says Sondheim, "there was no resonance" to some of these names "except to American historians" - which made the prospect of a high-profile British production of *Assassins* doubly brave. On the other hand, physical and emotional distance, so the thinking went, could be a very real ally to a show that had fallen foul of bad timing in New York. John Weidman was Sondheim's book writer on *Assassins* as he had been earlier on *Pacific Overtures*, and he remembers the cool initial response to a show that was fearless enough to cast a sidelong glance towards America at the precise moment that the Gulf War was stirring up national sentiment. One New York reviewer wrote that the proper thing under the circumstances was for *Assassins* to be closed down, as if, says Weidman, "what we were doing was unpatriotic and offensive." Others felt that the material was too serious to be treated within the genre of musical theatre - the very form that Sondheim had already reinvented countless times before.

It was hardly a surprise, accordingly, when *Assassins* failed to transfer to Broadway, especially since then-New York Times chief theatre critic Frank Rich had faulted the score's "stop-and-go gait and sometimes collegiate humour." (Hardly the salable quotes from which Broadway hits are made.) But if the subject matter was possibly out of step with the prevailing temperament of the time, there was the added feeling that an over-busy staging from the usually admired director Jerry Zaks hadn't best argued the show's case. As a result, the Donmar from Mendes' very first production there was ideally poised to do what it has done so often since: reconsider a contemporary show in the terms most capable of revealing the material anew.

"It really seemed like the right people in the right place," says Weidman, looking back on the Donmar's offer to do a show whose reception in New York had left him and Sondheim "reeling." Sondheim echoes his appreciation of a choice of opening that "was very speculative and very daring of Sam." Possibly working against the project, says Sondheim, was "the business of [English audiences]

Ciaran Hinds in *Assassins* ▶

having an emotional response to what is, essentially, a foreign event: that was one thing." On the other hand, Sondheim was well aware that there was the potential for *Assassins* "to be about a kind of America Britain would understand." Says Mendes: "There was no question in my mind that a British audience would absolutely understand it - if I got it right."

> **"I knew the theatre from its RSC incarnation. It's a great theatre to watch a show in and bloody difficult to design in, although I always have a good time going there. It's such an audience-friendly space, but I don't think it's a designer's theatre. It certainly is a performer's theatre. With everyone at the Donmar, there's a certain kind of democracy that comes into view with people who would normally be asking for their trailers and, instead, have to muck in and can't do anything about it: it's one for all and all for one. "**
>
> **BOB CROWLEY**, designer
> Into the Woods, 1998
> Orpheus Descending, 2000

In Mendes' view, so sketch-like a piece of theatre needed a fluency that had gone missing Off-Broadway. From that came the idea of a carnival or fairground setting to link both the scenes and the nine assassins, successful or otherwise, each of whom had his or her own booth that was lit from within. Above the stage could be seen a gun-toting Uncle Sam in accordance with the musical's thesis: that America's supposedly invaluable emphasis on liberty came at a price, allowing a citizenry committed to the right to bear arms the equal right to kill a president. "I think Stephen [Sondheim] was very pleased, probably, that we didn't get bogged down in literalism," designer Anthony Ward says of the production's look. For Mendes, what was crucial was a visual aesthetic which, as with the material itself, "the audience would get in the first two minutes - a truly dark sense of Schadenfreude, which was to say a black cabaret told in a style that hovered a foot above reality."

Mendes encouraged the show's creators to reassess what they had done in New York, even if, says John Weidman, more rewrites were considered for London than were ever actually implemented. Still, if there were changes to be made, now was the time. And for Sondheim, that meant incorporating a new song called "Something Just Broke," about the national grief in the aftershock of the Kennedy assassination. Unambiguous in its power and intention, the song laid bare the trauma that the satire in *Assassins* was otherwise sometimes content to keep at bay. The composer had intended the number for the Broadway transfer that never happened, so London afforded the ideal opportunity to insert it. Mendes couldn't have been more pleased. "I thought, if we're going to do *Assassins*, the show needs to pull the rug out from under you at the end: stylistically, we've now encapsulated in revue form the lives - the sanity and the madness - of these people, so now you have to say, 'Could this really have happened?' You needed a song in which everything was stripped away." "Something Just Broke" proved its adaptability nine years later: rewritten to acknowledge the events just gone of September 11, the song resurfaced on October 26, 2001, at the National Theatre in London where it made for a tremulous first-act finale to that afternoon's celebratory NT25 Chain Play.

Sondheim had written new material for London versions of his shows before: "Our Little World," the duet between the Witch and Rapunzel, was first heard in Richard Jones' West End premiere of *Into the Woods*, while the 1987 West End premiere of *Follies* had a host of numbers that were new to that version

Adrian Lester, the Olivier Award-winning star of *Company* ▶

of the show. And when the National did *A Little Night Music* in 1995, Patricia Hodge's Charlotte benefitted from a reinstated song, "My Husband the Pig," that had been cut the first time round on Broadway. Jeremy Sams was musical director on *Assassins* and remembers being the first person to receive "Something Just Broke" across his fax machine. "Stephen was going through a sad phase, and suddenly here was this amazingly beautiful and potent number. It was very, very personal." Although Sondheim had originally intended the song to be placed early in the show, Mendes persuaded him to let it become the musical's eleven o'clock number. As sung by the so-called bystanders, "Something Just Broke" locked into place the show's seriousness of purpose; what may have seemed glib or inchoate in New York now seemed alternately mournful and passionate, the new song anchoring in direct and grievous terms the sense of requiem that underpins the piece.

What was needed, of course, was a cast that could deliver material from which they might well have felt alien - and at an address where they would be happy earning £200 a week. *Assassins* auditionees included a virtually unknown Ewan McGregor. (*Trainspotting* was still four years away.) "He was very handsome," says casting director Anne McNulty, "in a sparkly-eyed kind of way." James Nesbitt came along and "sang beautifully," says McNulty, "but not to Sondheim's standard, or certainly not then." Eventually, as has always been true of Donmar musicals, an ensemble was arrived at mixing self-described novices like Ciaran Hinds with veterans of the genre: among them, Louise Gold, Michael Cantwell, and Henry Goodman, whose jaunty Charles Guiteau (the Garfield killer, seen in *Assassins*

highstepping his way to the gallows) later won him an Olivier. "I'd never been in a musical before," says Hinds, "and probably never will be again" - even if his part as the would-be Nixon assassin Samuel Byck demanded vocally only that he join in two chorus numbers. Says Hinds: "I think they recognised I'm not a singer."

At the same time, Mendes was showing the way in which an actor's experience of the classics - Hinds had played Achilles in the director's RSC *Troilus and Cressida* - could serve a musical with a strong text (an idea that subsequently would come to even greater fruition with Adrian Lester in *Company*). As

played by Hinds, Byck seemed a crazed variant on Travis Bickle from *Taxi Driver*, the film whose teenage star, Jodie Foster, had in fact prompted an abortive presidential assassination all its own. "Ciaran had these stonking great monologues, which he did brilliantly," says castmate Louise Gold: so what if singing wasn't his strongest suit? Sondheim, says Gold, who had played Gussie in a Leicester production earlier that same year of *Merrily We Roll Along*, "always prefers actors to singers; he would rather the feeling was right than someone just stuck rigidly to the notes in some perfect way." (In addition, the London version's eight-person band allowed for a more lustrous sound than the musical trio that had been employed in New York.) And so *Assassins* began previews October 22, 1992, opening to the press a week later. With its premiere was ushered in a decisive era in the history of British musical performance whereby Broadway glitz could be replaced by a studio theatre's ability to strike at the best musicals' bruised and sometimes savage hearts. The National's Cottesloe auditorium revival of *Sweeney Todd* the next season would further the same argument across the river.

The critics seemed more than ready to go where Mendes, Sondheim and co. were unafraid to lead. "This inaugural production takes perfect aim," wrote the Independent's Paul Taylor, a sentiment echoed by Irving Wardle in that paper's Sunday edition: "Sam Mendes gives a supple expressive line to a show that could easily fall into intricate fragments... From every point of view, Mendes' arrival in Earlham Street is good news." Praising a show that was "superlatively acted (and) powerfully sung," the Standard's Nicholas de Jongh had no patience for the fact that *Assassins* Off-Broadway "mightily flopped. Here it looks set for victory." John Weidman looks back on the run as "a satisfying and restorative experience" that helped reposition the show. Since then, *Assassins* has already had two small if well-regarded London revivals and is done on American college campuses all the time. Only in New York have the vagaries of timing conspired against it yet again: a Broadway premiere planned for autumn, 2001, had to be called off by the events of September 11. After the slaughter in New York of that momentous day, how could *Assassins* in good conscience get revived? (In the event, the cancellation was not for keeps:

▲ Stephen Sondheim

the Roundabout Theatre plans to return to the show in the 2003-4 season, with Joe Mantello directing.)

At the Donmar, there was significant pleasure taken in a production that had been undertaken on its own terms, free of the implicit commercial pressures - the will-it-won't-it-move? drama - that had hung over the same show's debut in New York. At Playwrights Horizons, says Jeremy Sams, who had seen *Assassins* there, "it was a mini-Broadway show. The one at the Donmar wasn't that at all: it was simply the thing itself, and of course it worked beautifully." Sondheim seconds the notion. "That was the great pleasure of the Donmar. I never felt that I would sink them or that anything depended on the show except doing the production well." And though John Weidman is the first to admit that commercial expectations for *Assassins* in New York have always been modest - "even in our wildest dreams, we never thought *Assassins* was going to push *Cats* out of the Winter Garden" (that task was left to *Mamma Mia!*) - the show's London run, he says, took place free of any ancillary angst. "I certainly felt as though we were mounting the show at the Donmar." And that was that.

In any case, Mendes' production was testing the Donmar every bit as much as the Donmar was giving a home to the show. *Assassins*, its company stage manager Nick Frankfort remembers thinking at the time, "was this enormous event that felt too big for this tiny theatre; doing a musical in that space was quite awe-inspiring." So, says Caro Newling, was her realisation early on of both the macro and microcosmic aspects of her job. The former involved dealing with Sondheim's agent, Flora Roberts, a formidable but also immensely smart and sympathetic woman (since dead). Newling had never done major licence agreements before

> **"The pleasure of the Donmar is the same pleasure of Playwrights Horizons in New York: since these are not-for-profit theatres, you just put on a piece and do it as well as you can without having any guilty obligation toward backers. That's what has been great about the Donmar: I never felt I would sink them or that anything depended on it, except doing the production well.**
> **Is the Donmar my London home? I think that's too sentimental. I feel that way about both the National Theatre and the Donmar; I suppose I can be sentimental on both fronts. The point is, Sam and his cohorts liked these four shows, so they put them on. As with *Nine* and *The Fix*, they put on what they like."**
>
> **STEPHEN SONDHEIM**, composer
> Assassins, 1992
> Company, 1995
> Into the Woods, 1998
> Merrily We Roll Along, 2000

working first with Roberts and then, a year later, with Bridget Aschenberg on the complexities of *Cabaret*. Both women, says Newling, "invested hugely in what Sam was about," while offering a fledgling administrator like Newling a model way of working. Flora Roberts "had that wonderful thing about never being patronising and being tough as old boots at the same time," says Newling. " I absolutely adored her and Bridget; they were so generous." Equally, Newling was discovering first-hand the sorts of specific demands that get made when you're running a theatre - as became clear one night when Sondheim came running in to report heatedly that there was no soap in the gentlemen's loo.

Housekeeping matters aside, one can't imagine a better representative than *Assassins* of what the Donmar and Mendes, both together and separately, would go on to do. The production's uncompromising subject matter - during one performance, some visiting Americans stormed out demanding that the theatre be bombed - would lend it what Mendes calls "that edge of controversy" that carried over in different ways to *Cabaret*, *The Blue Room*, and his work on screen. (*Road To Perdition*, with its seemingly limitless body count, could almost be called *Assassins 2*.) At the same time, it forged a connection with a composer through whose work the Donmar would come to know itself. "Imagine if *Assassins* had been a flop," muses Mendes. Let's not.

In fact, *Assassins* played to 97% capacity and made a profit of £5,706: the only show of that opening season to end up in the black. By the time of the Donmar's next Sondheim venture - *Company*, which opened just over three years after *Assassins* - the composer wouldn't simply be on his way toward becoming a house regular; he was offering a lifeline to a playhouse that in the intervening period had been having a parlous financial time. Throughout those years, the theatre had enjoyed the support - emotionally and financially - of George Biggs and Roger Wingate, who had been more than willing to underwrite the Donmar to the tune of several hundred thousand pounds but clearly could not and would not be able to do so forever.

> **❝ At the Donmar, you get a real sense of the company of actors; there is no star, no major glorious leading player. You get this group - this company - who are going to do the show for an audience in front and on two sides, and you can't really hide. You're out there and naked in front of them; it's a great space to perform in. Some of the most intimate things in *Company*, I felt, were very very easily communicated to people the furthest away from the stage. That's a great weight off your back as an actor, because the closer someone is, the easier it is to be truthful. ❞**
>
> **ADRIAN LESTER**, actor
> Company, 1995

It was far from obvious, however, who or where else could supply the necessary funds, especially since the Donmar was failing to emerge as a way station on the path to West End profits - which was, says Biggs, "really partly the reason why we started it; we were always looking for product." "*Translations* in the West End?" Mendes says of the Brian Friel revival that was an artistic high point of his first year: "That would have been pretty dodgy." On the face of it, the theatre might have seemed attractive as a commercial seedbed. But it became evident early on that few Donmar productions were truly capable of flourishing away from home. Says Roger Wingate: "There are not many shows that lend themselves to being transplanted from a 250-seat space" - which may explain why more Donmar shows have underperformed in the West End (*Design For Living*, *Lobby Hero*, and, indeed, *Company*, among them) than have seen their success repeated. (*The Glass Menagerie* and *The Real Thing* are two that did). That is also why in 1995 Wingate and

Mendes made a direct cap-in-hand appeal to the Arts Council. "It wasn't grandstanding," says Wingate, "and it did result in an emergency payment" - £150,000, a sum achieved early in 1996 with the staunch support of Thelma Holt, then chairman of the Arts Council's drama panel. After three years, says Caro Newling, "we could go into battle and fight for our survival based on what we had done so far." And the fight could, slowly and incrementally and not without difficulty, be won.

Still, Mendes knew that the funding eyes would be focused on the Donmar as it began its fourth season with *Company*. As it was, the theatre had turned an overall profit in only the second of its first three years, the halfway house between the worlds of the subsidised and commercial theatres proving a

Mark Thompson's Mondrian-esque SoHo loft in *Company* ▶

tough one to inhabit. On a purely aesthetic front, *Company* posed a separate challenge that came with its status as a widely known Broadway classic dating back to 1970 and to an original Harold Prince-Michael Bennett collaboration that went on to play in London at Her Majesty's in 1972 for the best part of a year. That meant that any new *Company* was competing with what is always the trickiest aspect of the theatre - an audience's collective, much-cherished memories of one of the signature shows of an era. And so a large part of the revival's success would surely depend upon the performer chosen to play Bobby, the determined Manhattan bachelor at the elusive core of Sondheim's great and tearing score. It was for that role that the Donmar - in a genuine casting coup - chose a Shakespearean actor who had never before carried a musical in a performance that carved out its own bit of history: Adrian Lester became the first black male on either side of the Atlantic to play the lead in a major production of a Sondheim show.

Colour-blind casting already had a welcome precedent in London musical revivals from around the same time: Clive Rowe - a fellow member of the *Company* company - had been an Olivier nominee in 1993 for his sweet and soaringly sung Mr. Snow in Nicholas Hytner's National Theatre *Carousel*. Nominated the next year was Lester himself, for his portrayal of the lovesick young sailor, Anthony Hope, in another National revival: Sondheim's own *Sweeney Todd*. "I'd worked with Adrian in *Sweeney* and thought he was pretty terrific," says the composer, who was the first to note that Lester's voice had strengthened in the two years between *Sweeney* and *Company*. The actor's greater achievement was to restore Bobby to the centre of a show from which he can sometimes seem a cryptic non-presence at his own 35th birthday party. No worries of that here: as directed by Mendes, this *Company* honoured the irony of the title. The show is about nothing less than loneliness.

The point of going with Lester was to write skin colour out of the equation: this wasn't so much a black Bobby as it was a Bobby who happened to be black. And as Lester remembers it, race wasn't the concern; it was the youthfulness of a performer who was only 27 at the time. "I said to Sam, 'I think I'm

too young,' and he said, 'Get over that.' He didn't want to cast some 50-year-old and ask him to play 35. Sam wanted someone who looked as if he was moving into manhood but wasn't quite," which Lester managed with the help of a light beard and a hairline shaved further back. "My wife hated it," says Lester. "She called me 'Odd Bod.'"

In truth, Lester wasn't Mendes' first choice for the part: that had been Iain

▲ Bob Crowley's set for *Into the Woods*, directed by the designer's younger brother, John

Glen, who declined the project in order to make some money in the West End starring for Cameron Mackintosh in the musical, *Martin Guerre*. "I'm not musically very informed," Glen says of *Company*. "I listened to the music, and it didn't really grab me." (Glen later got a second chance to work with Mendes when *The Blue Room* came round.) On the one hand, Mendes was fully aware that Lester's presence lifted what the director calls "the white middle-class chic New York curse, which is the thing that above all dates *Company* most." More important, however, was the haunted, yearning, immensely likable centre-stage presence that Lester was in the show: a pot-smoking, hip-swivelling bisexual who was the life of the party and yet in some essential way existed alone and apart. By the time the large-eyed performer got to "Being Alive," Bobby's eleventh-hour assertion of self, gone was any sense of a seminal Sondheim anthem as a ready-made rabble-rouser. That version of "Being Alive," Mendes notes with absolute accuracy, "had been sung at too many AIDS benefits: the song is not about *staying* alive; it's about the thing that makes you *feel* alive, which is other people." As happened at the Donmar in a different way with the title number in *Cabaret*, a vaunted Broadway classic here became a hymn to desperation and need.

There aren't that many moments in Donmar history that everyone who was in the building at the time separately relates; one of them is of a teary Sondheim making his way up into the theatre's offices following *Company*'s first preview, immensely moved by what he had just seen. "Steve couldn't speak," says Mendes. "It was absolutely wonderful to watch." A bachelor at the time, the director felt his own pull towards a piece about making connections - or perhaps not. "*Company* was about a young man at the same time of life as myself; it was a very individual response, and Bobby was the reason I did it." An admiring Sondheim speaks of "Sam's inventiveness in addition to the intimacy of the Donmar that made all the difference in terms of another view of the piece. Each character in *Company* is one you are supposed to be interested in and recognise." (It was difficult not to notice Clive Rowe's karate-obsessed Harry, who, the actor laughs, "used to be afraid that I would fall on [colleague] Rebecca Front and crush her; I had this horrible image of one of Britain's leading comedy performers being stretcher-ed out.") The material prospered under the microscope that is the Donmar while in no way supplanting Prince's justly celebrated original. "It's just nice to get another director's take," says Sondheim, and that was what Mendes duly offered up, abetted by a designer, Mark Thompson, who reimagined the musical in smart Mondrian-esque patterns that didn't need a skyline in order to scream 'Manhattan.' ("I'm rather against skylines, "says Thompson, who did put a Bombay skyline in *Bombay Dreams*: that city's verticality, however, is hardly the visual cliché that New York's has become.) Among the ensemble, Sophie Thompson and an Olivier Award-winning Sheila Gish made their own vivid impressions as two of the more memorably neurotic and impassioned women in Bobby's midst among a cast that, says Mendes, "treated [the show] as a coherent narrative, not just as pieces of music."

Company sold out its run and was taped for TV, like *Cabaret* before it. But just as the original West End version of the show ended up losing £62,000 of what in 1972 had cost £70,000 to put on, producer Bill Kenwright's commercial transfer to the Albery in 1996 failed to pay back a capitalization that had more than tripled in the intervening decades. Still, the legacy of *Company* remains an important one on the road to economic recovery for a theatre that had by then broken free of the Wingate-Biggs financial watch. By the time of the next Sondheim show, *Into the Woods*, three years later, the Donmar had benefitted from a major Arts Council appraisal and seen its staff go from five to twelve, an increase that brought with it a marketing officer and fundraising department that could devote itself to issues of cash. "That was the way it should be," says Caro Newling, mindful not to let theatre staffing grow too large.

"We're 250 seats, so if the administration goes beyond the size and scale of the space, that's where the axis gets tipped and becomes more about the ethos of the administration than about what's going on stage." *Company*, then, was crucial in showing that here was a theatre worth safeguarding, while *Into the Woods* came that much further along in the life of a regime carefully finding its own financial way out of the forest.

For all its cumulative kudos over time, *Company* had been twenty-three years between major London airings, and Mendes - not unusually for this director - had devised his own way in to the material: the entire show was happening in Bobby's SoHo loft. "He walks through the door, the room is empty, and in that moment of realisation of his aloneness, Bobby reconstructs and relives his relationships with his friends." *Into the Woods*, conversely, had been seen in London not ten years before, in a fiercely eccentric and adult production - directed by Richard Jones - that had an abortive run at the Phoenix Theatre where it was an apparent casualty of the Gulf War. The swift reappearance of the musical didn't bother its composer: "As far as I'm concerned, a good show should be revived every year." More surprising was finding one of Sondheim's most populous - *Into the Woods* has a cast of eighteen - and scenically complicated musicals braving the confines of the Donmar. As Sondheim remembers a concern of his at the time, "How were they going to get the Witch to transform at the Donmar, except by having her duck behind a tree?"

> **"The Donmar is a fantastic space if you get it right and an unforgiving space if you can't deal with it. It feels intimate in a play; it feels like the audience have sat in your lap at a cabaret. That front row is so close and the whole environment shrinks down; you feel like every little thing you're doing is under a kind of scrutiny.**
> **Sam has no fear, or should I say he transmits no fear. He never seems to come with any baggage or walk into any situation where he projects doubt. His tenure has been phenomenal but so has that of the team around him. It takes a great general to win a battle, but he has to have the soldiers."**

CLIVE ROWE, actor
Company, 1995
Divas At the Donmar, 2000 and 2001

The solutions fell to the brothers Crowley: John, the director, here staging his first-ever musical, and Bob, sixteen years John's senior, the Tony Award-winning designer who knew the Donmar well from its various prior incarnations. John Crowley had lost his Sondheim virginity, as it were, to Richard Jones' imagistic and unapologetically cruel West End production: "It had a huge impact on me; I just thought it was glorious." Eight years later, returning to the same musical this time as a director, John had learned the perhaps paradoxical fact that "the bigger the piece, the better the [Donmar] space would respond." (That belief was borne out even more so in his 2001 revival of *Tales From Hollywood*, in which the same director brought a minimalist majesty to what had once been a large-scale National Theatre epic.) The elder Crowley, Bob, was himself intent on the "incredibly liberating" process of distilling *Into the Woods'* visual essence: lights to suggest the different houses; a table and a mop and broom to distinguish the separate living environments of, respectively, the Baker and Cinderella; a two-foot-wide revolve (tiny in stage terms) for the fairy tale characters' various journeys. The woods themselves were a miniature receding forest from which Rapunzel's tower could be seen poking through. In the second act a pair of smashed glasses offered visible evidence of the frightening onward march of the musical's (unseen) Giant. The set, in John Crowley's view, was like a Joseph Cornell box, "full of surprises."

This musical had traditionally been blessed in its casts. Bernadette Peters and Joanna Gleason were the Witch and the Baker's Wife the first time round in New York (the show was subsequently revived on Broadway in April, 2002); Julia McKenzie and Imelda Staunton inherited the same roles in London. Early casting considerations at the Donmar floated some comparable names, starting with Patti LuPone as the Witch and Hugh Jackman and Philip Quast as the two Princes. ("I had done it in Australia," says Quast, explaining why he declined. "There was nothing really to be gained.") In the end, the vocal distinctions were shared by Nick Holder's portly and confidently sung Baker and the deliciously cheeky Red Riding Hood of a then-17-year-old Sheridan Smith, a part that the Doncaster native delivered in her own Northern tones. (Not a few American tourists mistook her for a Cockney.) And yet, if the singing wasn't the occasion - of all the Sondheim shows at this venue, *Into the Woods* was unquestionably the least well-sung - the Donmar by this point was savvy enough to let the acting and John Crowley's imagination rule the day. "It was very nice," says Crowley of his production's guiding virtue, "to see the stories released."

That approach suited its creators just fine. The show's book writer, James Lapine, recalls "really loving Sophie Thompson," who, like Staunton before her, ended up winning an Olivier for playing the Baker's Wife. And having presided over two separate and sizable Broadway productions within fifteen years, Lapine admired various directorial decisions taken at the Donmar - an ingenious shadow play for Little Red and the Wolf, for instance, or the wanderings through and round the audience of Frank Middlemass's Narrator. Sondheim, in turn, discovered an unexpected chamber quality to a show that can look big but is generally scored for just one, two or three people. (*Into the Woods* has only three chorus numbers.) As for the singing? "The world is not full of people," says the composer, " who can sing and act equally well: you always have to lean in one direction or another." Adds Sondheim: "In my opinion, I would rather lean toward the actor, particularly in an intimate setting where you're not having to project as much. It's in a big theatre, as soon as the non-singers start pushing, that you notice the voice is frayed."

John Crowley, for his part, was discovering the highly impassioned climate of the Sondheim enthusiasts, a world of which he had been entirely ignorant. At the first preview, Crowley recalls, "they were whooping it up after every song. I wasn't prepared for it, and nobody had warned me; that was a bit of a trip." The attention carried over to the Internet where the director found himself the subject of a piece on the Sondheim website - "and my jaw dropped." But if it was almost a rite of passage for every Donmar associate director to have his day with Sondheim (David Leveaux was mentioned for a *Pacific*

> **"** I had known the old Donmar, which was always great and I loved going there and it was kind of an OK space. But Sam has turned it into something very special without being fazed by it for a second; that's his enormous skill.
> If you've been playing large theatres, the intimacy can come as a bit of a shock.
> On the first night of *Assassins*, it was a bit scary: virtually the entire audience were critics or Judi Dench or Kathleen Turner. I thought, could there be some ordinary people in the audience? Because of the place it's become, you get some non-representative audiences. **"**
>
> **LOUISE GOLD**, actress
> Assassins, 1992

Overtures in the winter of 1999 that didn't happen, though that musical was eventually scheduled to reach the Donmar in the summer of 2003), the theatre's next go-round with this composer allowed another house regular, Michael Grandage, to make his full-fledged musical debut. *Merrily We Roll Along* didn't mark entirely unknown territory: a one-time actor himself, Grandage had assisted the American director Walter Bobbie on the West End musical *Chicago* and had been responsible for putting Maria Friedman and Nicola Hughes, the show's second pair of stars, into the production at the Adelphi Theatre. But with *Merrily*, Grandage found a successful way into a Sondheim musical that had been marked by repeated failure: the show could work, it seemed, if one honoured both its soaring music and melancholy undertow of pain.

Mendes had wanted for years to produce *Merrily* at the Donmar, where Matthew Warchus and, indeed, Crowley were talked about as possible directors for it at different times. Why such interest in the show? *Merrily*, says Mendes, "has attained a legendary status, but unless you're a Sondheim diehard, you won't have seen it at all." Beyond its fleeting appearances in Britain, the musical adaptation of George S. Kaufman and Moss Hart's 1934 play had resurfaced on the West Coast, directed by James Lapine, in 1985; at the Arena Stage in Washington DC in 1990; and Off-Broadway under the auspices of the York Theatre Company in 1994. British productions had been less high-profile and were confined mostly to amateur versions or late-night concerts. "It has always had this fascination hanging over it of this sort of brilliant score and difficult narrative." Like *Assassins*, this show brought with it what Mendes describes as "a challenge aspect" that he felt - and rightly - Grandage could meet.

Grandage had been a student at the Central School of Speech and Drama in 1983 when *Merrily* was having its London premiere under the auspices of another drama school, the Guildhall, a student production that Grandage saw twice. Seventeen years later, how was he planning to approach material that by this point seemed to have more versions than *Hamlet* has quartos? ("The comparison," says Sondheim, "is not inaccurate.") Grandage's idea was to use the 1981 script with a few additions to tell a story that had kept Sondheim and George Furth tinkering ever since the show's premature Broadway demise: the move backwards across twenty three years from adult disaffection (and, in one case, chronic drunkenness) in 1980 to the shared optimism of youth and of an America that was in so many ways still innocent in 1957. Grandage's attachment to the original *Merrily* somewhat surprised Sondheim, who only found out in rehearsal that Grandage wasn't doing the fully revised version of the show. That meant keeping the framing device of a graduation - the show beginning and ending with kids on the cusp of adulthood - that Sondheim and Furth later got rid of in their rewrites. Says Grandage, "I really really was impressed by how little Steve imposed on me, actually. He constantly said, 'Listen, this is your production, as long as you're clear about what you want to do.'" (Furth wasn't quite as sanguine but didn't interfere.)

The first problem was which version to use. The second was casting a musical requiring its performers to be consistently convincing as the years roll further and further back to the Sputnik-era exuberance atop a New York roof where *Merrily We Roll Along* ends. On Broadway in 1981, the decision had been taken to cast actual kids (*Seinfeld*'s Jason Alexander among them): the move, cruelly exposing, made about as much sense as that first production's ugly jungle gym set or costumes that consisted mostly of sweatshirts announcing who the characters were. Subsequent American stagings had cast adult

Julian Ovenden in rehearsal with Olivier Award-winner Samantha Spiro (top) for *Merrily We Roll Along* and in performance with Mary Stockley and fellow Olivier winner Daniel Evans (front) ▶

actors - and why not, with the bookending device of the graduation now gone? In restoring a framework to the action (and, with it, the song "Rich and Happy," instead of a subsequent Sondheim composition, "That Frank"), Grandage cannily took the middle way in a casting process that, everyone agrees, was not easy.

"It was a very fascinating experience," says Anne McNulty, "because Michael had never done a musical, and my experience of casting musicals was greater than his experience of directing them. So you kind of go, 'I know what I'm doing, and you have seen the best singers and the best actors.' It was not without its anxieties." Of the three leads (the cast numbers fifteen people in total), the first two to be cast went on to win Olivier Awards. To play Charley Kringas, the lyricist who remains true to his art even as he loses his best friend, the Donmar chose Daniel Evans, fresh from playing the title role in the National Theatre's *Candide*. Mary, the musical's female pivot, went to Samantha Spiro, who had earlier the same year played Celia in *As You Like It* for Grandage at the Crucible, Sheffield, and then at the Lyric Hammersmith in London. Spiro was worried that she might be too old, for one thing, and unable to do choreographer Peter Darling's steps, for another, and, additionally, not fully up to the score. (The role requires a mid-range up to high D.) In the end, it was the musical director Gareth Valentine who swung the role in Spiro's favour. As Grandage remembers it, "Gareth said, 'It's not one of the greatest voices, but it's one of those voices that will break your heart.'"

The real difficulty lay in casting the show's most slippery part: Franklin Shepard, the gifted composer whose betrayal across the years of his friends and lovers (not to mention of himself) has taken him to the top of the showbiz ladder but at a palpable and painful price. Kevin McKidd, the Glaswegian co-star of *Trainspotting*, had the voice

and certainly the talent but not the requisite look to play an all-American boy; others who came in and out of view for the role included TV's eventual Hornblower, Welsh actor Ioan Gruffudd. In the end, Grandage after seven meetings gave the role to Julian Ovenden, a 24-year-old tenor and former cathedral chorister who had played a herald in the final scene of the Yukio Ninagawa-Nigel Hawthorne *King Lear*. "When Julian laughs," says Grandage, "his entire face and body open up." And so a musical once derided by some as a wallow in caddish self-pity became a wrenching analysis of what it means not to be bad (which Franklin isn't) but weak (which he is). Ovenden, says Sondheim, "gave a much underappreciated performance, not to mention the fact that he played the piano" - a useful asset in a small theatre where faking it is not an option. "I thought he was wonderful."

So did critics and audiences of *Merrily* all told, which suggested that a London public may have been better conditioned than on Broadway to the properties of a musical whose structure is more commonly found in English drama: Pinter, Stoppard, and Ayckbourn are among those who have written plays containing the retroactive sting embedded in *Merrily*'s backward narrative. At the Donmar, it was hard not to bleed for Evans' frazzled, frizzy-haired Charley as he sang of a good thing "going / going / gone," as if mirroring exactly the course of his friendship with Franklin. On "Growing Up," Ovenden turned one of the show's more plaintive numbers into an argument with his own divided self. Spiro shed some cleverly concealed padding as she gained in open-faced adoration of Franklin while the years rewound: though vocal problems sidelined Spiro for three-and-a-half performances during previews (she did half of one show before being urged by Sondheim to go home), her acting never lost its pitch. Nor did the musicality of an evening that gained from entirely new (and pricey) reorchestrations for a nine-person band by Jonathan Tunick, arguably the most esteemed of Sondheim orchestrators.

The show played through the winter to more than 96%, where it remains, says Grandage, "of all the productions I've directed, the one I've gone back to see the most." (That was partly, he admits, out of a tendency to want to fiddle.) Its eventual victory at the Oliviers trumped not just Cameron Mackintosh (*The Witches of Eastwick*) and Andrew Lloyd Webber (*The Beautiful Game*) but belatedly secured *Merrily*'s reputation for keeps. Grandage's reaction to the win: "I sort of nearly died," says the director, who was in rehearsal that day so got the news via a text message on his mobile phone. "All I could think was how angry that would have made a lot of people." Sondheim deflects the attention back to the qualities of his musicals as plays. With *Merrily*, he says, "you think, 'Here's a traditional musical,' but the fact George [Furth] has written it makes it a play." In all his libretti, says Sondheim, "the characters are much more interesting than in most musicals and deeply drawn and full of light and shade because I work with playwrights, capital P."

It helps to have been paired with three directors over four shows with whom this composer has felt as if he were in tune. "Sam has an instinct for musicals. He comes from a deep love of them, and you have to love the genre in order to take them seriously. John Crowley loves musicals, and, listen, my guess is that Michael Grandage would like to be in a musical." Sondheim goes on: "Doing shows in England is my idea of terrific." The Donmar, one can safely assume, hasn't finished repaying the compliment.

In rehearsal: Associate directors John Crowley (top left), David Leveaux (top right) and Michael Grandage, who is Sam Mendes' successor as artistic director ▶

willkommen

america, part 1
- the musicals

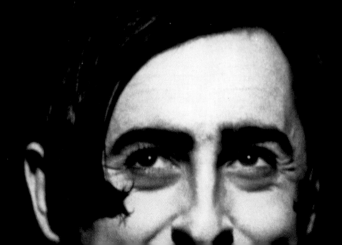

chapter 3

Stephen Sondheim is so regularly produced in England that it's tempting to think of him as an honorary Brit. But the maestro was hardly the sole American represented at the Donmar during the Mendes years.

Even in New York, one would be hard-pressed to find a not-for-profit theatre that within ten years has staged four works of Sondheim, three from both Sam Shepard and David Mamet, and two each by Richard Greenberg and Tennessee Williams, with Paula Vogel, Lillian Hellman, and Maury Yeston among the American theatre artists that have each seen defining works boldly reimagined. (The 2002 American season - a phenomenon in itself - is discussed in the final chapter.)

Why such a westward-looking emphasis? Mendes, like Richard Eyre a generation before, had grown up steeped in American movies and plays, with the result that he felt to some extent as if he knew America before he ever got there. In fact, Mendes only first visited New York in 1992 to see Dearbhla Molloy (whom he had directed at the Young Vic the previous year in *The Plough and the Stars*) on Broadway in Brian Friel's *Dancing At Lughnasa*. The director arrived in Manhattan not a complete newcomer to America, having done a brief teaching stint in Tampa, Florida, that his Chichester boss, John Gale, had helped organise. During that time, he managed to attend that year's Super Bowl final, complete with screen images of George Bush Sr. and jets flying protectively low over the stadium. "I thought I'd woken up in [Orwell's] '1984,'" says Mendes. "It was quite spooky."

Florida, he says wryly, "I didn't find massively attractive." But Manhattan was a different story: "I loved New York the moment I got there." Mendes' affinity for things American would go on to be seen in his choice of movies, an English theatre director announcing himself as a filmmaker with two quintessentially American works. "What America offers, and I think this is key, is that one's sense of the mythic is always much more present there than in England." Consider, for instance, the deliberate placelessness of *American Beauty*'s opening shot. That, Mendes points out, "by definition is saying, 'Any town, any street, anywhere in America'. You put it in England, and the audience goes, 'Oh, I think I know that house.' Or, 'where's the sea?' I love this country, but one's feeling is of a small narrow island surrounded by water."

The American theatre has no shortage of stories possessed of a certain metaphoric dimension and weight. In a myth-making category all its own is the monumental iconography of the American musical, starting with *Gypsy*, which is to bring Mendes back to Broadway in spring, 2003. Not to mention the

Broadway musical classic that turned out to be this director's calling card to Hollywood: *Cabaret*.

John Kander and Fred Ebb's watershed collaboration of 1966 had been groundbreaking from the start, both in its choice of subject matter (Weimar Germany in the early days of the Third Reich) and in a staging from director Harold Prince and designer Boris Aronson that raised the bar on Broadway at the time: New York Times critic Walter Kerr wrote in his original review of a "style driven like glistening nails into the musical numbers." While English expat Sally Bowles invited an audience to "come hear the music play," the musical itself was sounding the more dissonant notes of a civilisation nearing collapse, its decadent amorality first embodied on stage and screen by Joel Grey's supremely epicene Emcee. Aronson's now-historic design coupled a visual riff on painter George Grosz with a large mirror - later paid homage to in the Donmar design - reflecting the audience back on itself. The implication: no one was immune from the nightmarish slide into the abyss that this musical dared to anatomise.

The first *Cabaret* ran 1165 performances at Broadway's Broadhurst Theatre. The subsequent 1972 Bob Fosse film, featuring an Americanised Sally Bowles in Liza Minnelli, won eight Oscars. And there was Mendes late in 1993 revisiting the musical's literary sources (Christopher Isherwood's *Berlin Stories*, an account of his years in Germany between 1929 and 1932, and John van Druten's 1952 play, *I Am A Camera*) while acknowledging - though in no way imitating - both the original stage show and the movie. The attempt, says the director, was to come to grips with the "extraordinary cocktail" that is *Cabaret*, with Mendes quick to concede that his revival might well have ended up shaken but unstirred.

"That show could have come and gone very quickly and quite unimpressively," Mendes says of the first of what would be a Donmar series of Christmas musicals. Instead, playing to 106% (standing room included) over sixteen weeks, it became the transforming production of the Donmar's early period just as *The Blue Room* in turn was five years on. The revival's New York version early in 1998 not only marked Mendes' American directing debut - followed a month later by his National Theatre *Othello* at the Brooklyn Academy of Music as part of a world tour - but brought him to the attention of Steven Spielberg and DreamWorks. From that, of course, were *American Beauty* and Mendes' career as a film director born.

In New York, Mendes felt surrounded by icons: Minnelli and Grey, Prince and Fosse, choreographer Ron Field. "I remember thinking, 'Blimey, in terms of shared cultural knowledge of a show, *Cabaret* comes pretty high up the scale because, in fact, of the movie.'" Back in London, he had thought of the material as any director steeped in the classics well might. *Cabaret*, Mendes says, was "up there with *The Crucible* or *The Homecoming* or any other play of the twentieth century that deserves to be reinvented and rediscovered generation to generation: it's a great piece of theatre."

How, then, to communicate it anew - especially in a West End that had hosted a dismal revival of the piece during the 1980s, with Wayne Sleep as a fairly desultory Emcee? Mendes found his answer in a discovery that he had made several years into directing, "I think I realised in the theatre that it wasn't enough to like a play or simply feel like you could make it work; you have to ultimately feel like you have a secret about the play. A secret that only you have and that, in the end, you make available to the audience." That unique way in to *Cabaret* lay in the environment in which it would be presented: by turning the stalls of the Donmar into the Kit Kat Klub, performer and spectator alike were made complicit in the poisonous seductions of an age poised for collapse.

"The idea itself wasn't new," John Kander says of Mendes' directorial conceit. What was, the composer

Two Olivier Award-winners: Sheila Gish (top) in *Company* and Sophie Thompson in *Into the Woods* ▶

maintains, "was that kind of talent and imagination. When *Cabaret* was first done, it was fresh and imaginative and no one had ever seen anything like it. And in a funny way, that's what Sam did for a whole other generation: we got back the feeling *Cabaret* had had the first time out."

This was achieved by re-examining the original from scratch and playing about with Joe Masteroff's book in a way that would continue further once the revival reached Broadway. Pictures by Grosz and his German contemporary Otto Dix were pinned to the rehearsal room walls. (It didn't hurt that the Tate Gallery had housed a major Dix retrospective in spring, 1992.) Mendes had the cast read Fred Ebb's lyrics for a long while without singing them. Chorus members were encouraged to write their own character's histories, while a visit from Isherwood's writer-friend and colleague Stephen Spender helped the *Cabaret* performers understand the mores of the time. Spender, says Mendes, "talked very gently about life in coffee bars and cafes and how to pick up boys, and he was equally gently encouraged by Alan [Cumming]." The session provided a useful backdrop to a version of Masteroff's book that would point up the bisexuality of Sally Bowles's American admirer Cliff (played at the Donmar by Adam Godley, who quickly became the solid anchor of an exceedingly lively company). Musical director Paddy Cunneen was kept busy teaching nine members of the ensemble to double as musicians capable of joining the four principal players of the show's Kit Kat Band. The actor playing Ernst doubled up on banjo, while Fraulein Kost showed an unexpected talent for the violin. In musicianship terms, "the Germanic roughness and drive came from Paddy," says an admiring Mendes, who thinks back on *Cabaret* rehearsals as "five weeks of a kind of crazy freedom." The stage itself was reduced on all sides by about a metre, the bench seating in the stalls replaced for that production only by tables and chairs. "If this is a club, then it's a working environment," says Mendes, who wanted a *Cabaret* in which the audience, too, would have to work.

The Donmar leads, Jane Horrocks and Alan Cumming, each felt differing degrees of pressure, Horrocks was dating Mendes at the time, having got an Olivier nomination for his production of *The Rise and Fall of Little Voice*. That performance had required her to parrot the legendary vocals of numerous divas, among them Liza Minnelli's mother, Judy Garland - and thereby linking the role of 'LV' in *Little Voice* directly to *Cabaret*. "I don't think I've ever worked with someone I was

> " I actually think it's a deceptive space in that it's bigger than you think; when watching as an audience member, you think you couldn't get any closer if you tried, but being on stage it's a much bigger space than you think it is. Certainly vocally you have to be careful to get to the back upstairs because the space goes right up, and you have to be aware of this higher level. You have to get the voice up and the eyes up.
> It is a small big space, if you like. The size takes away that kind of fear - if you ever have it - of the audience member breathing down your neck because you know the space is quite big enough to handle it. At the same time, you can reach out to people: you can pick them and look at them and use that. The other thing is when a show there is working, you do actually physically feel it; you know you have given people that experience, and it's immensely satisfying.
> I've worked there three times.
> How lucky am I? "

JENNY GALLOWAY, actress
Nine, 1996
Electra, 1997
How I Learned To Drive, 1998

currently going out with either before or since," says Mendes, who was worried that " people might think Jane was there because of me. I felt protective of her." Horrocks, in turn, reports feeling "a bit dubious about *Cabaret*" despite confidence in "Sam's ability to pull it off and direct me in the correct way." Were her doubts a result of the legacy of Liza? To some extent, and also: "I've always been dubious about being in stuff that has been done before; I much prefer new work where you're not judged against anybody else." Nor did she want the performance simply to be about the quite astonishing party trick that had distinguished her star turn in *Little Voice*. That same talent for mimicry found the actress soon able to take off nearly the entire Donmar staff - except one, says Caro Newling, sounding a note of quiet triumph: "Jane did brilliant impersonations of everybody, but she couldn't get me."

Cumming had in fact made his London stage debut at the Donmar in 1988 under its previous regime (his Victor and Barry double-act with Forbes Masson was part of the Perrier Pick of the Fringe). And there he was again, having graduated to, of all parts, Hamlet in a touring production that Mendes had booked into the Donmar immediately prior to *Cabaret*. As a result, Cumming wasn't at all sure about rehearsing the Emcee by day and playing Hamlet by night. "I knew I would just be sort of a wreck and that every musical theatre actor in London would hate me and want to kill me. Here's this fabulous prime role that comes up once every decade, and it was being taken by a straight actor." He laughs. "Such a hilarious phrase."

More seriously, Cumming recalls telling Mendes, "I don't do musicals; they're not my bag. I don't really want to - the Emcee, yuck. I had a problem, and still sort of do, about ending a sentence and bursting into song." It took serious heeding of his director's intended approach for Cumming to warm to the idea. "I came back to Sam and said, 'Look, if I'm going to do this, I really want it to be proper - not shlocky or musical theatre-y, but the way it was done at the time.'" From that arose the image that prevails on Broadway still of an entirely dark theatre brought eerily to life by the Emcee's eyes. At once Cumming saw the way in which the Emcee could be "almost the eyes of the audience, luring them in at the very beginning and yet challenging them once they're in." And so the performer signed for a show that would over time find him forsaking his Crouch End flat for American renown. And serving for four months as the Donmar's resident prankster.

Before long, Cumming stories were rife. Jane Horrocks remembers the night, during her first-act number "Perfectly Marvellous," when she inadvertently switched the verses round, which left her having to "la la la" her way through the second verse. On stage throughout the performance, a gleefully unforgiving Cumming proceeded to make hay of the mishap by reintroducing her as "Fraulein Sally Bowles - la la la." Throughout the run, Horrocks had to deal with the upstaging tendencies of a co-star whom she had first met on the set in Wales of a little-seen William Hurt film called *Second Best*. "It started off," she remembers, "where Alan just sat there quietly, and by the end of the run he was practically masturbating during your scene; it was slightly irritating." It may have been partly his love of the spotlight on stage that explained the actor's reluctance to opt for a theatre job off it: in 1995 Mendes encouraged Cumming to direct Ken Stott in a Donmar revival of *Tartuffe* - in a new version by Scottish writer Liz Lochhead - but the project never got off the ground.

Mendes, meanwhile, had looked on amazed as Cumming completely improvised the production's much-celebrated sequence at the end of the Entr'Acte when the Emcee picks

Cabaret's two Sally Bowles: Jane Horrocks in London and Natasha Richardson, who won a Tony for her performance, on Broadway ▶

someone from the audience to dance. From a very casual feeling of "let's try this" at the first preview, the gesture became a signature part of the show, with Cumming's dance partners over time including, in London, critic Mark Steyn and BBC weatherman Ian McGaskill and, on Broadway, Mikhail Baryshnikov and newsreader Walter Cronkite. Liza Minnelli saw the production on various occasions on Broadway but Cumming left her in peace: "It doesn't really work with celebrities, I found." What did work was the show's appeal to an A-list crowd that Cumming was quick to chronicle. "Alan used to write a list of the famous people who'd been in," says Horrocks, "and we had to add to the list."

It was in New York that Mendes' vision for *Cabaret* was fully realised, joining David Leveaux's transplanted *Electra* among the ventures first seen at the Donmar that came into their own on Broadway. In London, Cumming's pansexual charisma aside, the production was chiefly notable for offering the Olivier Award-winning Sara Kestelman the role of her career as Fraülein Schneider, the Jewish landlady who gets two standout numbers: "So What?" and "What Would You Do?" (Off stage, Kestelman made a somewhat separate impression when she demanded that the music at the closing night party be turned down.) When Kestelman seized the spotlight, you forgave the absence from the production of an essential Broadway razzmatazz. With Kestelman, the Donmar's capacity for cutting to a show's ultimately shocking quick was startlingly clear, as a musical once allied to vocal bravura came to seem instead a study in isolation and loss. And in the sometimes horrific march of history.

The London staging survives as the first Donmar production to be taped for television. (*Company* was the next). What's more, says Caro Newling, " it was the turning point for everybody; with *Cabaret*, we hit our stride. Now, if we did *The Life of Stuff*" - the Simon Donald play from Mendes' first season that played to 35% - "we'd be sold out. We did a lot of early work assuming a knowledge about the Donmar that wasn't there." That was until *Cabaret*, after which few could be unaware of a small theatre's potentially sizable clout. And of a production that remains the best-attended of the Mendes years.

Cabaret continued its salutary stride abroad. The Broadway run opened under the auspices of New York's not-for-profit Roundabout Theatre at the Henry Miller Theatre on March 19, 1998, winning four Tony Awards that June, Cumming's best actor trophy among them. That November it moved to Studio 54, where, as of this writing, it is still playing after 1800 performances - one of the few Broadway revivals to have outrun the original. In London, one felt that, though totally game, Horrocks wasn't entirely up to the reconception of a Sally Bowles so blind to events around her that the title number - far from seeming anthemic in the Minnelli manner - became a frantic *cri de coeur*. (Natasha Richardson took over the role on Broadway.) Horrocks talks of spitting out "Cabaret" the song so that it was "a bit like Sid Vicious. Under John Kander's instruction, I might add." Mendes does his own altogether affectionate imitation of Horrocks making her way through "Mein Herr."

On Broadway, the show may have gained from the gathering anticipation that came with opening some thirteen months late, the delay prompted by problems pertaining to a "found" venue (the Supper Club on West 47th Street) that was abandoned in the end. But it was worth the wait and more to see Cumming take total command of an American audience in the city he would soon be calling home. (And Mendes a second home: it was while rehearsing the show late in 1997 that he began renting his Greenwich Village flat.) "I didn't grow up thinking the theatre could make you famous," says Cumming. He was astonished that a stage run - opposite four separate Sally Bowles over time - could lead to TV and film success, beginning with the Julie Taymor movie, *Titus*, that Cumming filmed during a break from *Cabaret*. (Small world department: Mendes lost the *Cabaret* Tony for best director to Taymor, for her work on *The Lion King*.) Cumming continues: "What *Cabaret* did for me in America was massive, and it's so weird for a play to do that." Weirder, too, for one person to turn into "this mascot for debauchery and sexuality" that, in his own words, the elfin provocateur soon became.

Horrocks didn't travel to New York with *Cabaret* and has, in fact, only done one play since: a controversial Greenwich Theatre *Macbeth*, opposite Mark Rylance. Instead, Mendes' Broadway staging had an immediate *raison d'être* apart from Cumming in the career-defining Sally of Natasha Richardson, whose mother, Vanessa Redgrave, had her own brief singing career in the film of *Camelot*. An English actress much-admired in New York, where she and husband Liam Neeson live, Richardson caught the self-delusion and pathos of a northern English mill owner's daughter aspiring towards reinvention as a Chelsea girl. And towards a blinkered heroism that in its way seemed mad. As Richardson delivered the title number, toppling the stage microphone in the process, the show found a moment in performance to go with its unusual milieu. "I'd always felt," says Mendes, "the song was a kind of suicide note about staying in a city that Sally knows is going to end in rubble." And so a one-time eleven o'clock hell raiser emerged as an unexpected thematic cousin to "Rose's Turn" from *Gypsy*: dual showstoppers functioning as acts of painful, nearly psychotic self-revelation.

Cabaret's New York success - Richardson, like Cumming, won a Tony - led inevitably to talk of a return London stand, this time to the West End. But Cumming wasn't overly keen on the idea of reprising a role he had by that point done on Broadway for well over a year. As for Mendes, "I absolutely said no to doing *Cabaret* again in the West End. At a certain point, it's just a money-making enterprise, and I'm just not interested." In any case, he adds, "the show has outlived any of our expectations" (including spawning an American tour that began in Los Angeles in February, 1999).

The Donmar production had seemed, says its director, "the beginning of a brilliant idea which I hadn't seen through. It was chaos, to be honest, but we got by with chutzpah and elan." In New York, working with the American choreographer Rob Marshall as both choreographer and co-director, Mendes added songs ("Maybe This Time," from the movie), reordered scenes, and rethought some less felicitous ideas. That explains jettisoning his original take on the giddily rapacious "Money" as a song about homelessness with Sally and the Emcee appearing in cardboard boxes. Deadpans Mendes: "It had got a little *too* Brechtian." Among the show's Broadway admirers was *Cabaret*'s original Emcee, Joel Grey: "For me, the production was all about John Kander and Fred Ebb and the fact that their brilliant score was up there able to withstand the challenge of a gang of gifted people seeing it through different eyes; what

> "It's just so fantastic to be able to do theatre like that and have the audience right up against you; I love it. When I did Hamlet's soliloquy, I could look at every single person; you feel like you're really connecting with the people who've come to see it. At the same time, the Donmar doesn't feel like a little theatre - even though there aren't very many people, it doesn't feel poky and cramped.
> Even in 1993 Sam was such a *wunderkind*. The thing that impressed me - and still does - is that he's so sort of organised and ordered in his work. He's always been sort of successful, Sam: he's brilliant in the sense that he's always had success and worked very well and not been daunted by things. It takes a really healthy attitude not to freak out about running a West End venue at age 10. "

ALAN CUMMING, actor
Hamlet, 1993 (visiting)
Cabaret, 1993

could be more flattering?" And though the Donmar receives no royalty from the show's Broadway run, its runaway success there - that Roundabout production has hosted over a dozen Sally Bowles to date - sparked the first of several profitable New York fundraisers for the Donmar. Held three days prior to that year's Tonys, the event earned the Donmar close to £90,000. And it launched an American awareness of the theatre that has not abated to this day.

> 66 **I was excited about the prospect of opening *Cabaret* in that production, so close to the audience, though I seem to recall the acoustics weren't that amazing: a lot of people at the top couldn't hear. That and *The Rise and Fall of Little Voice* were, I think, sort of the highlights of my theatre life. I used to see so much at the Donmar; I don't see anything anymore. 99**
>
> **JANE HORROCKS**, actress
> Cabaret, 1993

The Roundabout, in turn, learned to love the Donmar, inviting John Crowley to reconsider Off-Broadway (albeit in significantly different terms) his Donmar revival of *Juno and the Paycock*, with a new cast but retaining its London leading lady, Dearbhla Molloy. In March, 2003, New York is scheduled to get a second musical revival, *Nine*, in a Roundabout staging first seen in embryonic form at the Donmar late in 1996. And as with *Cabaret*, New York will have to give the Donmar credit for proving one essential fact: a musical's original Broadway incarnation, however acclaimed, need not be the final word.

No one in 1996 was more keen to find a totally new way in to *Nine* than its American composer-lyricist Maury Yeston, especially in a country he has long held in great affection. (After graduating from Yale, Yeston had been a Mellon fellow at Clare College, Cambridge, where he remembers David Pountney, Nicholas Hytner, and Clive James among those "busily doing things.") "I have lived for so many years in Europe and have such a love of other cultures," says Yeston, "that I loved the idea that other places might interpret my work in terms of who they are and what's relevant to them." Britain had tried to mount this musical before, with Daniel Massey and Jane Lapotaire at one point mentioned to star in one production and Ian Judge on tap to direct another. In the end, all that happened was a one-off CRUSAID charity performance at the Royal Festival Hall in 1992; Jonathan Pryce, Ann Crumb and Liliane Montevecchi (who had won a Tony for the show on Broadway) headed the gala cast.

And yet, just as *Cabaret* seemed not easily divorced from the Prince-Fosse imprimatur, so, too, was *Nine* wedded in many people's minds to director-choreographer Tommy Tune's 1982 Broadway premiere. Adapted from the Federico Fellini film *8½*, the New York debut of *Nine* was a ravishing exercise in chic, with twenty-one women elegantly draped around one man. The object of all that feminine attention was Raul Julia's Guido Contini, the filmmaker with a fatal flaw - his boundless appetite and love for women. And so, against stiff competition the same season from Michael Bennett's *Dreamgirls*, *Nine* won a handful of Tonys, included prizes for Yeston and the crucial Best Musical award. Fourteen years later, how could the tiny Donmar hope to compete?

The answer lay in a single word, Europe. While Mendes all along had hoped for a *Cabaret* that would seem more European in its leanings, Leveaux realised that geography could play a similar trump card with *Nine*. "I thought," says Leveaux, for whom *Nine* was both his first musical and his first production at

Alan Cumming in *Cabaret* ▶

the Donmar, "we'll try and get it a bit closer to Fellini because we're in Europe. So my way into the show was thinking, where does this connect - albeit not too solemnly - with the world of Fellini. And I don't think that's where Tommy [Tune, the director] had come at it at all; he came to it simply as a radical musical." Rather usefully, Leveaux had caught the New York production near the end of its run (by then, Bert Convy had replaced Julia as the self-styled Casanova, Guido) and had seen first-hand the defining chic of designer Lawrence Miller's tiered black-and-white set - a spectacular tiled affair at once elegant and forbidding. (Detractors likened it to a classy loo.)

"What I remembered," says Leveaux, " was this high-concept thing that Tommy had done in a Tommy Tune way; it had sort of impressed me, but I hadn't warmed to it." Softening the artiness of the Broadway version, Leveaux and designer Anthony Ward came up with a design dominated by a dining table surrounded by fourteen chairs (one for each woman in the London version's reduced cast) beneath a tilting, tarnished mirror. The stage floor was to flood with water during the hallucinatory second-act Grand Canal sequence, courtesy a four-foot wide trough built into the set by master carpenter Dominic Fraser. But if the floor, thankfully, was watertight, the casting of the demanding central part was not: few other Donmar productions threw up quite so many roadblocks in the search for the ideal star.

Filling the role now would be far simpler, says casting director Anne McNulty, who at the time had been considering an American lead for *Nine* only to bump up repeatedly against what McNulty remembers as "that thing of, 'And you're who?'" The production, she says, "happened in our fifth season, but our 'known-ness' as far as the American community and their willingness to acknowledge the possibility of coming to join us for a project had not really been established." Kevin Kline popped briefly

into the frame and very quickly out of it: the Juilliard - trained Oscar-winner isn't referred to in the business as Kevin "De-Kline" for nothing. Anthony Crivello, a swarthy Broadway veteran with something of the style and look of Raul Julia, was a more plausible bet and knew London (and the Donmar) from his West End appearance in 1992 in *Kiss of the Spiderwoman*. But he turned out to be otherwise engaged. "There was quite a lot of unavailability," says McNulty, who was also trying British actors. On that front, she came up against "a number of people we approached who at the time didn't want to do it." Martin Shaw, John Bowe, and Hugh Laurie were among those who disappeared swiftly from view. Jeremy Irons typed up a gracious thanks-but-no-thanks and sent it straight to Mendes.

In the end, "literally days away," says Leveaux, from the start of rehearsals, Marcello Mastroianni's screen role went to Larry Lamb, a tall, silver-haired West End performer who, like his director, was making his musical debut. Surrounding him were some pretty seasoned musical ladies - among them, Sara Kestelman, returning to the Donmar following *Cabaret* ; the clarion-voiced Susannah Fellows, a West End regular; and a short, squat powerhouse of a performer, Jenny Galloway, who walked away with the show. If Lamb didn't possess the vocal chops to compete, there was no denying his presence: the actor's lean, somewhat dissolute good looks combined with a pair of haunted eyes to suggest the adult in Guido struggling to emerge from the child. As much Peter Pan as Don Juan, Lamb was to that extent the right centrepiece for a musical that sets a reflective fortysomething against his nine-year-old self. (At the Donmar, three boys shared the Young Guido part.) And it was opposite the libidinally inclined young lad that a barefoot Galloway jolted the production into earthy and boisterous life, in the first act sending the whoring Saraghina's gutsy "Be Italian" through the Donmar roof. An elemental sand dance, the song was both great theatre and richly evocative of the film insofar as the fleshy Galloway deliberately recalled Edra Gale, Fellini's choice for the role.

Galloway looks back on the production as "absolutely thrilling: it was so wonderful to go down that spiral staircase and feel the audience go, 'How many more women are coming down the stairs?'" The quantity of ladies meant inevitable spillage backstage into the male dressing room, with, recalls Galloway, "a discreet curtain for Larry, I don't think that stayed drawn very long." And though Yeston shared in the general concern for Lamb's lungs - "Larry did the best he could, but he was not optimal vocally" - the composer was nonetheless seen weeping openly in delight through most of the press night. Yes, Leveaux had cut the opening song, "The Germans At the Spa," and forsaken many of Tune's most memorable flourishes, among them the body stocking for Carla, Guido's come-hither mistress, and an extravagantly long feather boa for his agent, Liliane La Fleur. But what the London director gave back to the show was a period style (in keeping with the 1960s provenance of *8½*, Clare Burt's Carla had about her the whiff of Marilyn Monroe) alongside a new sensualism and warmth. Previous productions in Sweden and France notwithstanding, Maury Yeston at last felt he was seeing his *Nine*: "It was the first time I had seen this piece done with the scent of Europe I had written into it."

Leveaux later restaged the production to acclaim in Argentina, where a Spanish-speaking company presumably came naturally by the musical's Latinate demands. Yeston speaks with pride of it winning "mejor musical" in Buenos Aires and of a local cast that "had so little trouble; the Argentinians are basically Italian." In keeping with that country's timetable, each performance would begin after 10.30pm and end well after midnight, following which the cast would go out and tango - rather a change from

Jenny Galloway as the whoring Saraghina in *Nine* ▶

bolting through Covent Garden to catch the last tube home. Back in London, Caro Newling took pleasure in writing to Yeston's New York agent, Flora Roberts, that her client's show was an Olivier nominee for best musical. But for all its aesthetic virtues, the show did sub-par business at the Donmar, and a lung infection sidelining Lamb (and necessitating a week of cancelled performances) didn't help when it came time to balance the books: "I think Larry found it quite difficult throughout the whole run," says theatre manager Julia Christie. "He never said the words, 'I enjoyed it.'" Forecast to play to 90%, *Nine* remains the only one of the Donmar's Christmas musicals to drop to an average of 73%.

Nine watched that year's Olivier Award go to a long-running West End money-loser, *Martin Guerre*, whose producer, Cameron Mackintosh, was to play a major part in the next American musical to play the Donmar: his co-production of *The Fix*. But unlike *Nine* or *Cabaret* or *Company, The Fix* was a world premiere - and the first time Sam Mendes had directed a musical from scratch. The two had worked together on an enormously lucrative 1994 Palladium revival of *Oliver!*, a project Mendes had undertaken not least to make some money in the commercial arena so he could continue working on a Donmar salary: "That production enabled me to stay at the Donmar; I don't think I could have afforded to otherwise."

Mackintosh had been involved with the Donmar from its very start, having put money into *Assassins*, and so thought of Mendes when a satiric American musical called *The Fix* crossed his desk. (Who knew

▲ Philip Quast (centre) won an Olivier Award for playing the polio-ridden uncle in *The Fix*

then that the show's sidelong glance toward a murderous America, a point of view at once grimly comic and doomy, would position *The Fix* somewhere between *Assassins* and *American Beauty* in the Mendes canon?) A tale of a Kennedy-like clan of political schemers, the show set its maladjusted America against a richly varied score suggestive of Frank Loesser one minute, Jimi Hendrix the next. "I had a sense that *The Fix* would appeal to Sam as something for the theatre," recalls Mackintosh, citing the director's ongoing attraction "to pieces that have a few dark corners to probe." And why not in turn, the producer argued, expose the musical's relatively unknown creators John Dempsey and Dana P. Rowe (their major credit prior to *The Fix* had been an Off-Broadway musical called *Zombie Prom*) "to a director of Sam's calibre and at the Donmar? John and Dana couldn't imagine better people in the theatre actually taking an interest in them and their work."

Mendes had seen the barnstorming musical *Rent* Off-Broadway in its very first incarnation at New York Theatre Workshop and had admired the "group energy which carried the piece through with all its flaws; it felt sort of passionately scattered across the stage." And he had a similar reaction to a tape of *Cal*, a musical named for its central character - would-be senator Cal Chandler - that would later change its title to *The Fix*. The semi-improvisatory feel of *Rent*, Mendes felt, carried over to *Cal*, alongside a score that "had a kaleidoscopic number of ideas; it was a kind of pop-culture grab bag." Without much delay, Mendes committed himself to Mackintosh and to that rare Donmar venture that had the West End (specifically, the Lyric Theatre) already in mind prior to opening night. Until, says Mackintosh, who ended up enhancing the Donmar staging to the tune of £300,000 (operational losses included), "we got reviews so deadly that there was no possibility of moving it."

"No flowers. No bouquets. Donations only to Talent Incorporated for better luck next time," sounded Michael Coveney's Daily Mail dirge. In The Sunday Times, John Peter blasted "the kind of preposterously self-important musical that Americans are so remorselessly good at." (One wonders if Peter has seen three or four of the British musical mainstays that wear self-importance like a badge of honour, but hey...) And so on: opening in May, 1997, twenty four hours prior to Disney's West End debut with *Beauty and the Beast* and the week after Tony Blair's first Labour landslide, *The Fix* found itself quite simply the wrong show in the wrong theatre at the wrong time. "No one wanted to be cynical about politics then," recalls the production's Olivier Award-winning star, Philip Quast, who was well aware of the vagaries of timing. "Since then, of course, we've had Monica [Lewinsky] and Bill [Clinton]; I think the critics just missed the point."

A Donmar misfire (the show averaged 70% attendance, well below expectation for Donmar musicals, if not their plays), *The Fix* achieved a partial vindication in its American premiere eleven months later at a suburban theatre near Washington DC, where director Eric Schaeffer refocused the material to warm reviews: as a result, Mackintosh then hired Schaeffer to direct Dempsey and Rowe's subsequent West End collaboration, *The Witches of Eastwick*. But even in London the production offered up a far more vibrantly eclectic score than is the West End norm, and it was beautifully served by a hard-working cast, headed by Quast as the musical's chief Machiavel - the crippled yet cunning Grahame, uncle to John Barrowman's Tom Cruise lookalike of a Cal. (Barrowman was an Olivier nominee, too.) The part of Grahame had been put the way of Henry Goodman, Jonathan Hyde, and Jonathan Pryce, among others, none of whom was available. But Mackintosh speaks of Quast as one who, uniquely, "had digested a combination of Richard III and Archie Rice and then spat it out; [the performance] was wonderfully tortured."

"I had one of the best times [during *The Fix*] that I've ever had," says Quast, recalling Barrowman's off-colour dressing room behaviour ("Sam would come in, and John would have his cock in my ear") alongside the antics of a director who treated his mechanised set like some enormous toy. "Sam loved to play with our manual revolve, making it go faster, and there I was on crutches for the part and Sam got some speed up on the revolve and he suddenly stopped it dead deliberately." What happened? Quast laughs at the memory: "I just went splat, absolutely, thinking, 'You fucking cunt.'" The part made real physical demands, too, on the 6'3" Australian with the shivery baritone voice. (In 2002, Quast returned to the Donmar as a thrillingly intense "diva".) "I realised I was rather too big and robust for someone who had polio," says the actor, who based one of the most remarkable moments of his performance in *The Fix* on a visit to the polio association. While there, a man fell over as he was showing Quast his calipers and then had to struggle to get into his wheelchair. Quast used the incident when it came time to do the show. "That was the great thing," he says about *The Fix* at the Donmar: "you could go over-the-top, and also play it for real."

> **The Donmar is just the most amazing, extraordinary space - it can take all the size that you want to give it: the biggest wide shots, but you can also play the tiniest close-up, like working on a film. There's something wonderful about a theatre where you realise audiences can see each other and that when you've got your back to someone, the audience behind you is getting what you're doing through the people on the other side.**
> **Once you've worked there, you're part of the family, which is what the RSC used to be in lots of ways; you are part of a team. And for £250 a week? It's impossible; you've got to save to go there. *The Fix* was a big cast, and I love the idea that all of us were on the same money because it makes it a true ensemble.**
> **What I like about Sam is that he's a bloke: he's just a down-to-earth person who has other outside interests. We went to the cricket together in Sydney during the millennium, and when you've got a person who actually can balance some other great passion and love, it makes it much easier for him to wear the mantle of director and producer, instead of just being completely obsessed.**

PHILIP QUAST, actor

The Fix, 1997
Divas at the Donmar, 2002

With hindsight, the creative team admit that *The Fix* may itself have been a shade too OTT. "You could have done *The Fix* without the doughnut revolve, the Vari*Lites, the technology: you really could have," says Caro Newling of a show that, she feels, "suddenly tilted toward Sam doing something on the scale of *Oliver!* in the Donmar; we were already carrying the West End in our heads, and that's not what we should have done." While acknowledging that a less slick staging might have served the material better, Mendes wonders at the same time whether *The Fix* wasn't an early example of the Donmar beset by its own success. "Here, you have critics looking at masterworks like *Company* and *Translations* in a small space, and when you put new works directly up against them, they have to be very good." He elaborates the point: "People have every right to expect the same experience from *The Fix* that they had at *Company*, but you're talking about one of the greatest musicals ever written and a new musical which

More Olivier winners: Sara Kestelman (top) in *Cabaret* with George Raistrick, and (below) Henry Goodman in *Assassins* ▶

is rough and ready and trying things that might not work. People want new musicals to be as good as the ones being revived." And fair enough, too: without good new musicals today, no Donmar or its equivalent will have shows to revive tomorrow.

Much the same problem hovered later that year over the only other entirely new musical - also American (albeit with a Canadian lyricist) - of the Mendes regime. Exactly a year earlier, *Enter the Guardsman* had won the top prize at the first International Musical of the Year competition in Aarhus, Denmark, beating out, among other shows, *Red Red Rose*, a musical about the Scottish poet Robert Burns that had incidentally showcased John Barrowman in the lead. No sooner had *Guardsman* lyricist Marion Adler, book writer Scott Wentworth (Adler's husband), and composer Craig Bohmler divvied up their £40,000 cash prize before offers arose for a full British production of a musical adaptation of Ferenc Molnar's *The Guardsman*. (In Denmark, the judges had awarded the winners based on director Julia McKenzie's staged excerpts from the shows.) Duncan Weldon was keen, citing the Chichester Festival Theatre - which he was then running - as a likely point of departure en route to the West End. No less interested was the Donmar, whose house ethos soon won over the creators of a backstage chamber musical featuring a cast of seven and band of eight. "Sam made us feel very at home," says Wentworth. "The Donmar is accustomed to having writers around. They're more in line with the process we're used to."

The director was Jeremy Sams, whom Wentworth and Adler had wanted from the start. "Scott and I had read a piece about Jeremy in Plays and Players," says Adler, "and had thought, we should be working with this guy; he speaks five languages, including German, which is one of the languages Molnar wrote in." And given that Molnar had, after all, written the play (*Liliom*) that led to *Carousel*, perhaps it was time for the Hungarian dramatist's inspirational potential to be shown anew. That explains how it was that the *Guardsman* team found itself installed in a Britain reeling from the death of Princess Diana - book writer Wentworth speaks of "that sense of being in a place where history was being made" - working on the full premiere of a musical, he says, about "how you keep a monogamous relationship eroticised." In the musical's abiding metaphor, a sustained, sexually satisfying marriage was very much like a long-running play.

Well, perhaps some texts just aren't lucky: Molnar's 1911 play itself went on to have a spectacularly short West End revival in autumn, 2000, with Michael Pennington and Greta Scacchi heading the cast. And with Alexander Hanson playing the actor who aims to reinvigorate his marriage by appearing before his actress-wife (played by Janie Dee, who later made a sizzling Donmar "diva," appearing in the same summer cabaret season as Quast) in disguise, *Enter the Guardsman* never generated the sense of rapture at the Donmar that had greeted it in Denmark. (That was notwithstanding eventual Olivier citations for the show itself and for Nicky Henson's supporting performance as a voyeuristic playwright and Molnar surrogate). Instead, the notices took a tone that could be characterised as "pleasant enough," to quote The Sunday Telegraph's John Gross. Susannah Clapp in The Observer felt its narrative was "classically witty, that's to say rather unpleasant" (so much for pleasant enough), while Alastair Macaulay in The Financial Times called the show "perfect in its way, and that way is to be awfully clever, light, and too pleased with itself." What fizzed in Denmark had become fatally arch.

In retrospect, Jeremy Sams says of a production that ended up playing to a dispiriting 49%, "it mystified me, *Enter the Guardsman*; nobody wanted to see it. I don't think ultimately it was a Donmar show." (Not that it made much more of a stir Off-Broadway several seasons later.) Presented with

£180,000 in backing from Andrew Lloyd Webber's Really Useful Group, which had the idea of sponsoring a new musical at the Donmar every season for three years in return for first refusal on any transfer, *Enter the Guardsman* turned out to be the first and only such venture in a scheme that soon evaporated - especially when such follow-up projects as a new Mendes-directed musical from Alex James of Blur never materialised.

"Again", says Mendes, citing issues of comparison raised by *The Fix*, "*Enter the Guardsman* was the victim of, 'Why isn't it Sondheim?'" And so he took a decision. "I just thought, look, at the end of the day this is the wrong place to premiere new musicals which are going to get punished for being new." Various Off-Broadway musicals emerged as possibilities for British launches (among them, Jeanine Tesori's *Violet* and Adam Guettel's *Floyd Collins*), but Mendes had by then learned his lesson. "Had we not caught a cold on *The Fix* and *Enter the Guardsman*, we would have done *Floyd Collins*," which not long after got performed at the Bridewell in any case. But the Donmar by that point "had become just slightly too big a venue," in terms, he says, of "both size and perception. You watch *Violet* and you say, well, it's not *Sweeney Todd*."

Rediscovery, Mendes had by then noticed, "is where this space is best used."

DONMAR

lit by lightning

america, part 2
- the plays

chapter 4

Mendes early in his regime began applying his credo of wholesale reconsideration not just to benchmark American musicals but to comparably important plays. And so it was that in the summer of 1994 he was reviving David Mamet's *Glengarry Glen Ross* while the impact of Bill Bryden's 1983 production of the same play was still fresh (at least in avid theatregoers' minds).

Wasn't the director tempting fate given the power of memory, not least as it hovers over major stagings of major plays? What's more, director James Foley's film version, with Al Pacino and Kevin Spacey, had not long been released, as Mendes was reminded when he bumped into Jonathan Pryce after the *Glengarry* revival's first night. "I told Jonathan I had just opened *Glengarry*, and he said, 'Why don't you just tell them to see the movie?' I thought, 'Thanks Jonathan,' who of course was in the movie. He looked at me as if I was absolutely mad." The director had taken on the play in part at the insistence of Caro Newling, whose attitude all along toward projects was, in Mendes' words, "if that is the one you want to do, then do it." Directorial passion, in other words, would always out.

Mendes thought he had a notion about the play distinct from Bryden's world premiere of eleven years before, a National Theatre staging that had set Mamet's real estate drama on course to its status as a Pulitzer Prize-winner and contemporary classic. (Broadway is set to revive the play in 2003, with Danny DeVito heading the cast.) Whereas Bryden's production, Mendes felt, had "its heart in the second act," the aim at the Donmar was to punch up the play's sense of threat in the Chinese restaurant duologues that make up the first act: the crime, as it were, followed post-interval by the punishment. The mounting dread animating Mamet's script was heightened in visual terms by the slow revolve of Johan Engels' set, a carefully realised if sometimes recalcitrant piece of machinery that prompted an interval scene change at the first preview of nearly forty-five minutes. ("I think we got it down to twenty-two," says Lucy Davies, Mendes' then-assistant.)

Glengarry was not easy to cast, and not only because Jack Shepherd's defining Richie Roma - Pacino's part in the film - had won him an Olivier Award a decade before. (The play itself won, too.) "It was a battle," says Anne McNulty, who remembers "the minefield" of saying to one prospective company member or another, "You're a senior actor, but we don't know if you can do an American accent." McNulty encountered "all kinds of bullet heads or hardheads who would say, 'Yes, I can do it; don't worry,' and I would say, 'I'm not worrying. I'm just saying I need to know you can do it.'" The result? "We got the cast we didn't know we wanted but we found," headed by Ron Cook as a scrappy yet sorrowful

◀ Helen Mirren

Roma and a moving if waywardly accented James Bolam - in an Olivier-nominated performance - as the play's most painful dupe, Shelly "the machine" Levene.

For Cook, the Glengarry revival marked a return to the theatre where he had first appeared more than a decade before with the RSC only to be back as part of an all-male company that was divided among the two dressing rooms on the basis of who smoked and who did not. A Geordie by birth, Cook would later get to act one in the Donmar premiere of Dusty Hughes' *Helpless*. (At the time, Cook wrote on the front of Hughes' script NAR - No Acting Required.) In *Glengarry*, the cast had to play Chicago real estate salesmen desperate for leads and peddling worthless Florida properties to buyers that were not necessarily as gullible as they seemed. How did Cook prepare for the job? "To help, David sent a tape in which he told dirty jokes with a Chicago accent," Cook says of Mamet, who was otherwise engaged during the production tending to a pregnant wife back home in the US. It wasn't long before Cook had so fully absorbed the part that he could tell off audience members in character. One night, noticing a pair of shoes encroaching into the playing space during the performance, Cook adopted his best Richie Roma snarl: "Get your fuckin' feet off the stage." The feet, Cook reports, were swiftly removed. On the final night the company gave a suitable backstage send off to Mendes, who was just then forsaking the Donmar to direct *Oliver!* in the West End. Imagine Mendes' surprise to find his Chicago hustlers belting out Lionel Bart's "I'd Do Anything," the "I" changed to "We."

The Donmar returned twice to the Mamet repertoire. Early in 2000, an American trio of actors headed by *Fargo*'s W.H. Macy in his British theatre debut opened a somewhat becalmed revival of *American Buffalo* in London before transferring director Neil Pepe's production (amid noticeably less favourable reviews) to Pepe's Off-Broadway base, the Atlantic Theatre in Chelsea. In a wild about face from *Mamma Mia!*, director Phyllida Lloyd followed up her surprise West End success trawling the back catalogue of ABBA with the London premiere at the Donmar in spring, 2001, of *Boston Marriage*. A decided anomaly in the Mamet canon - among other things, this most male of writers had never before written a play entirely for women - the play was at its core an exercise in mimesis: the master of demotic American speech turned epigrammatic wit as a modern-day Oscar Wilde or Noel Coward. The London premiere marked a bit of a coup following abortive attempts at a separate Broadway

> " I knew the Donmar before it was the "Donmar," when the RSC used it as their studio. It was very much a warehouse in those days, and the facilities weren't quite as good. With Sam taking over and doing classics and really good new work, it was very exciting. What I love is that the Donmar is very actor-friendly in a way in terms of the administration. It's so small that everyone seems to know you and you feel you belong to this small group of people who take an interest in you, with the theatre at the centre of it. Even when I go back now, they know you front of house and in the bar and in the administration. It's a very personal thing: you definitely feel you belong.
> Sometimes, I think my sort of mass increases as I get nearer the Donmar in a quantum mechanics way. At different periods of your life as an actor, you have different homes. The Donmar is one of my homes. "

RON COOK, actor
Glengarry Glen Ross, 1994
Juno and the Paycock, 1999
Helpless, 2000

Ron Cook in Glengarry Glen Ross ▶

production, to be directed by Howard Davies, that had been talked up for the likes of Sharon Stone and Anne Heche. In Britain, a choice trio of players was headed by Zoë Wanamaker, making her third Donmar appearance in five-and-a-half years. Alongside her were the gravely beautiful Anna Chancellor and young newcomer Lyndsey Marshal, who was later nominated for an Olivier for playing her senior colleagues' skittish Scottish maid.

Not surprisingly, *Boston Marriage* sold out at the Donmar, where it elicited some mixed and many excellent reviews, later transferring to the West End to satisfying if unspectacular business and mostly terrible reviews. "The second stringers murdered us," says Lloyd, who had been drawn to the script early on: "I thought, if anybody is going to make this work in England, I can." As was everyone who saw it, Lloyd was intrigued to find Mamet of all writers addressing Sapphic tendencies in a script with a faux-Restoration feel containing phrases like "Byronic rodomontade" one minute and deliberate anachronisms ("kiss my ass") the next: was the playwright having us on, or what? "Somebody had said to me that David had written a love story," says Lloyd. (Indeed, the title *Boston Marriage* derives from an arcane New England term for a long-term monogamous relationship between two unmarried women). "And I guess I felt that if the play wasn't underpinned with very high stakes, it would just be written off as a divertissement - which, oddly enough, the second time round it sort of was." The irony is that *Boston Marriage* remains one Donmar premiere collectively thought to have been enhanced by the shift out of the studio theatre to a larger, proscenium-arch venue. "We felt it had more detail in the West End, more heart," says Lloyd, " though I don't know that David wholly liked what we did in the end. Perhaps heart was the wrong thing to allow to creep into it; I don't know."

> **❝ I'd always known about the Donmar and always managed not to get a ticket, so it was new to me in every respect, though of course its reputation wasn't. That intimacy is nice, though I think the space is quite hard: just as I was settling into playing it, we were being moved on.**
>
> **You can see the audience, and they all seemed very rich - a sort of in crowd, or at least people who were very familiar with going to the theatre and listening.**
>
> **Stylish is the way to put it: Caro and Sam were always an incredibly stylish team to work for, incredibly welcoming and supportive. You get no money - hardly any - but they make up for it in every other way. They have this wonderful mixture of knowing how to treat people and being very egalitarian; they're very down to earth. ❞**

ANNA CHANCELLOR, actress
The Real Inspector Hound/Black Comedy
(Warehouse Productions), 1998
Boston Marriage, 2001

The text, says Anna Chancellor, "suited playing out in a proscenium because David had taken so much from writers like Coward who were written to be performed in those theatres." And whereas the Donmar audience, Chancellor says, "were all visible in their cashmere and pearls, we got a much more raucous crowd in the West End. When the dykes came, they would be laughing and laughing," which pleased Chancellor no end: "In a way, you want that mixture in your audience; you want different people to get different jokes." Looking back on "a tortuous rehearsal period," Zoë Wanamaker felt "we didn't find the play's style until it moved." *Boston Marriage*, she said, "worked best when we played it like a vaudeville but not quite. David wanted it to be real but also to have that feeling of just being presented." That may explain why the evening seemed both a comment on triviality and deeply trivial itself, as if its author were offering up an exercise in pastiche as opposed to those more personal Mamet plays that clearly originate somewhere deep within.

Besides Mamet, Sam Shepard was the other American writer given three separate Donmar airings, also to variable effect. The first, and far away the happiest, was Matthew Warchus' blazing revival of *True West*, one of the best-attended non-musicals of Mendes' early years. (Indeed, a measure of the situation the theatre would find itself up against financially was that a production playing to a commendable 87% capacity could still lose money - albeit only £1,275.) Hot on the heels of his scabrous premiere during Mendes' first season of Simon Donald's gleefully bloody *The Life of Stuff*, Warchus was back with a production of *True West* (done in collaboration with the West Yorkshire Playhouse in Leeds) that was really two plays in one: in a drama about the shifting power struggle and merging identities between brothers, Warchus decided to have performers Mark Rylance and Michael Rudko alternate roles. And why not, insofar as their characters, Lee and Austin, were Janus-faced halves of one changeable and volatile whole? So volatile, in fact, that Rachel Weisz recalls cowering as she watched the play: "I sat in the corner and hid. That's what the Donmar can do - make you feel like

❝I've been very lucky to have worked for a small clutch of producers, as in artistic directors, who just have the most extraordinary skills of empowering other people to do the job. In no way do you feel that Sam is looking over your shoulder telling you what to do, although, like Stephen Daldry, they would both be able to talk you into selling your granny.

I'm always seeing the impediment to why I'm either not worthy to do the thing or why I can't get off the starting block. Sam has this ridiculous ability to clear the path in front of you and make you feel: If anybody can do this, you can. Even though you know in this profession that there's a strong element of bullshit, somehow you know at the Donmar that you're not going to get dumped in it. It was six years between *Threepenny Opera* and *Boston Marriage*, by which time the theatre seemed cosmetically different, in that there was the presence of Hollywood on the block and the sense that Sam's life was expanding hugely. But I would have said the essence of the place was completely unchanged: there was the same informality, the same lack of pretension. That's very much a tribute to Sam's relationship to Caro and the rest of the staff: Caro's tireless energy and spirit and generosity and enthusiasm are what have kept the thing on track.❞

PHYLLIDA LLOYD, director
The Threepenny Opera, 1994
Boston Marriage, 2001

you're just there in the room." Not to be outdone was a younger generation that got its own charge from the play (or, at least, from a crucial set of props): Caro Newling remembers her godchildren, aged three and seven at the time, staring transfixed at the row of toasters that every night made possible the production's most violently funny set piece.

The male leads' swapping of roles every three or four performances - the performers playing the show's two other characters remained constant - made for high drama behind the scenes, as well. "It was a gruelling experience, doing that," Warchus recalls of a directorial idea that "really preys on and exaggerates the natural insecurities of a rehearsal process enormously: whilst each actor is trying to find

> ❝ I did *Piaf* there for the RSC when it was the Warehouse, and Peter Whelan's first play, and then we all thought it was going to disappear, so the fact that it was turned back into a theatrical space was great. I like seeing stuff at the Donmar: it feels like a good rehearsal room and isn't pretentious, and there's something about it which is like a studio. As far as the acting, you still have to use the same amount of voice as you would in a proscenium arch; it's quite deceptive in that way.
>
> Caro and Sam are very caring and have created a great team. They have great taste, and they don't push. Sam, I think, is a joy to work with; I really do. ❞

ZOË WANAMAKER, actress
The Glass Menagerie, 1995
Electra, 1997
Boston Marriage, 2001

Zoë Wanamaker: A favourite "Donmarine"

▲ Ben Chaplin and Zoë Wanamaker in
The Glass Menagerie

his own way through the play, he's watching another actor go through the same process and find things that he may have been missing. It's a great opportunity for paranoia." And yet, the benefits were as clear to the production as was its shift in England from the 800-seat Quarry Theatre in Leeds, where the revival had begun, to a London home seating less than one-third that number. Usually with plays, says Warchus, you're moving from a smaller venue to a larger one, so you have "the challenge of trying to find a new amplification of energy." With *True West*, the task was reversed: Coming from a large auditorium into the Donmar, he says, "played into the effect of blasting the audience into the three walls of the theatre."

True West had been seen before in London to a rather more muted response at the National late in 1981, where John Schlesinger directed Antony Sher and Bob Hoskins as the near-fratricidal siblings, one brother as reined-in and precise as the other was unruly and ready to

▲ Zoë Wanamaker, Lyndsey Marshal and
Anna Chancellor in *Boston Marriage*

Zoë Wanamaker in *Electra* ▶

snap. Thirteen years on, Warchus' gloves-off staging catapulted the text to the very front of the Shepard canon and six years later earned the director his second Tony nomination when the play was remounted with an American cast on Broadway. In New York, Shepard's play was regarded as near-sacred terrain following its galvanic presence Off-Broadway in the early 1980s with Steppenwolf Theatre Company regulars John Malkovich and Gary Sinise in the leads. Stepping where few might therefore choose to tread, the actors in Warchus' American revival, Philip Seymour Hoffman and John C. Reilly, staked out their own claim on the singular frontier of a playwright for whom the American west isn't half as wild as the brutish landscape occupied by humankind.

> **The theatre's reputation had grown with Sam, and, of course, it was great being in the centre of town. So *Orpheus Descending* was something I very much wanted to do, and it's just easier to do a play like that - any play, really - in such a small theatre.**
> **It's not an ideal space - far from it. You think you can do the equivalent of film acting and then you realise you have to look up; you don't just want the audience seeing the top of your head. Like any theatre, it has advantages and disadvantages, so you make the best of what you've got. And although they pay you fuck-all, that's a part of the experience, too. When it comes to doing theatre, actors subsidise their own work all the time.**
> **Every night backstage after the show, we'd have a bottle of champagne or, more often, two: people would take turns bringing a bottle in. I can't remember whose idea it was, but it was accepted and gladly embraced. The best fun was we used to stick the champagne corks into the dressing room wall so that future companies would look up and say, 'I bet that cast had a good time.' I wonder if the corks are still there.**
>
> **HELEN MIRREN**, actress
> Orpheus Descending, 2000

The terrain isn't dissimilar in a subsequent Shepard play, *Fool For Love*, which reconfigures the battleground for two lovers, Eddie and May. (Ed Harris was the original Off-Broadway Eddie.) Revived at the Donmar two years after *True West*, *Fool For Love* made for a significantly less charged evening in Ian Brown's underpowered revival of a play that Mendes had "really wanted to do myself and gave away." Earlier in 1996, Brown's Traverse Theatre production of *Bondagers* had transferred from Edinburgh to the Donmar to fine reviews as part of the admirable Four Corners season devoted to visiting companies from around the UK. Brown's work on Sue Glover's play had impressed Mendes, "and I thought Ian was the man for the job." Instead, says Mendes, "for one reason or another it didn't work. Sometimes that's what happens." Sometimes other things happen, too: one day, theatre manager Julia Christie entered the auditorium to find that all the surrounding litter that was a part of Robin Don's raised platform of a set had been cleared away by José Frias, the theatre's Portuguese cleaner. Says Christie: "He's never touched anything on stage ever since."

Fool For Love's leading man Finbar Lynch, making the second of his three Donmar appearances, this time as the explosive Eddie, regarded the production's failure to attract an audience as a test the Donmar passed in triumph. "In some theatres, you would feel abandoned; people would look the other way when they saw you coming down the corridor." Not here. "Caro and Anne were in regularly," Lynch reports, further remembering one particular matinee when a woman well into her 70s stood and applauded a dismally attended performance. At such moments, says the actor, "you just kind of think, it doesn't matter we're not doing great business as long as somebody thinks it was worth coming in."

Heaven knows what those audiences thought who saw Wilson Milam's misbegotten Donmar revival in the summer of 2001 of Shepard's *A Lie of the Mind*, the leisurely and highly poetic play that had been thoughtfully served by Simon Curtis in its Royal Court premiere fourteen years before. Hampered by a cramped set ill-suited to the Donmar space, the production by all accounts was as unhappy away from the stage as it looked awkward on it. The show made history of sorts as the only one of Mendes' regime to so demoralise theatre employees that Caro Newling finally had to tell Milam, the director, that his behaviour would not do. "It was the first time ever that a director has come into our building and I have systematically watched every single person try and try to deliver to him and be mentally abused."

Newling snapped one day when Milam announced that he and leading lady Sinead Cusack were going shopping for a new chair for the set in the absence of a suitable one from the company manager. "I just went off my head with anger," says Newling, "knowing the level to which those people can deliver and watching the entire Donmar staff lose faith in everything they were doing - and in the show." And afterwards? "Wilson never came near me again," says Newling. "I think he snuck into the building a couple of times to see the actors."

That such an anecdote stands out speaks volumes about a regime capable of calling the shots when things aren't going well while mindful on other occasions not to confuse public clamour for a show (or not) with artistic merit. In 1998, the theatre took great pride in snaring the British premiere of Paula Vogel's Pulitzer Prize-winning *How I Learned To Drive* and equal pleasure again in John Crowley's production of it. Vogel had been knocking around the American theatre through

> "I've always loved the Donmar from the first time I went there as a child, or the first time I consciously remember going, which was to see the Druid Theatre's *Playboy of the Western World* when I must have been about 13. It was just a magical night, and I've loved it ever since. I'm not a fan of big theatres, and at the Donmar, you feel people right on top of you; you're very aware of the audience. I'm sure it varies from actor to actor, and that there are certain corners that are your least favourites. But it's a magical place to go and see a play; it's a magical place to be in a play.
>
> I've only been in a play there once, but I feel like I'm part of the family. They all just make you feel so special. It's my favourite theatre in England: long may it continue."

BEN CHAPLIN, actor ▼
The Glass Menagerie, 1995

twenty-two plays but had never before had so sizable a New York hit. Perhaps unexpectedly, her eventual success came with an account of the none too healthily burgeoning relationship over time between a physically precocious American southerner, Li'l Bit, and the oversolicitous Uncle Peck, who teaches the girl to drive - and rather more. Off-Broadway, the play survived numerous cast changes - various Li'l Bits included Mary-Louise Parker and Molly Ringwald - en route to a film sale for a movie that has yet to be made. So the indices were good when Crowley chose *How I Learned To Drive* as the first American play he would direct in London, with Helen McCrory and Kevin Whately as Li'l Bit and Uncle Peck. So it is fair to say that no one was prepared when the critics ran Vogel off the road, much to the chagrin of a creative team convinced (and rightly so) that they had been wronged.

It may be that the first-night reviewers didn't like Vogel's refusal to sensationalise the issues: amid an attitude toward paedophilia in Britain that had been building toward the truly shameful name-and-shame tactics of the tabloid press, Vogel's reluctance to demonise her characters no doubt looked like the easy option; in fact, her mature perspective was that much more hard-won. Or maybe the critical

indifference simply lay in an adverse reaction caused by too much fanfare. (Tellingly, when another Pulitzer Prize-winner, *Proof*, arrived at the theatre nearly four years later, its laurels were kept out of all publicity and print ads.) In any case, *How I Learned To Drive* remains the best Donmar production to have done (at 43%, having been budgeted at 50%) the least good business, Vogel's highly sophisticated view of her traumatic subject caught at every turn by a far more shadowy and disturbing staging than

▲ Jenny Galloway and Helen McCrory in rehearsal for *How I Learned To Drive*

had been the case in New York. "One critic complained that Li'l Bit and Uncle Peck don't even sleep together, so it's not real abuse," recalls Crowley. Four years later he is still dismayed at the literal-mindedness of the "appalling" response to a play that Vogel had at the time compared to *Murmur of the Heart*, Louis Malle's shimmering 1971 film about an older woman's affections for a fourteen-year-old boy. "It seemed that if you weren't Mamet or Miller or Shepard, you were going to get short shrift in London as an American playwright," says Crowley - an estimation, accurate at the time, that subsequent American seasons at the Donmar have done much to emend.

"It was a human story," says Jenny Galloway, who completed a Donmar hat trick by following *Nine* and *Electra* with a terrific double as Li'l Bit's mother and aunt. "Maybe [critics] just didn't listen to the whole story." None of which mattered compared, says Galloway, to the fact that "we knew what we were dealing with; we knew what the material was - how fantastic it was - and we'd all fallen in love with Paula anyway; we wanted to do her proud." In doing precisely that, the production cannot be separated from a simply tremendous performance from McCrory that made clear the way in which survival in life is so easily accompanied by scars. Shifting in age from her early teens to nearly forty and back again, McCrory honoured every step on Li'l Bit's journey toward a forgiveness that nonetheless found her unable to forget. Because as Li'l Bit, says the actress, "you engaged with the audience straight away, people were as engaged whether it was a full house or a small one." Which may also be McCrory's modest way of deflecting praise where it is due: the actress - later to return in Mendes' final Donmar pairing of shows, playing Olivia and Yelena - grabbed the wheel of the play and, to coopt Li'l Bit's own language, floored it.

The revue-like nature of *How I Learned To Drive* coexisted happily with a brooding poetry that the theatre's two Tennessee Williams revivals tapped into directly. Nicholas Hytner may have seemed as rash in 2000 to tackle *Orpheus Descending* as Mendes had been six years before in taking on *Glengarry Glen Ross*: like *Glengarry*, Williams' difficult yet rapturous text remained strongly linked with a production from the recent past - namely, Peter Hall's first foray into the West End after running the National, with Vanessa Redgrave fairly ablaze as Williams' lovesick Lady. That account of the play did sellout business at the Haymarket in 1988 before moving on to Broadway, where it proved that Redgrave - who had been considered commercial anathema in New York because of her anti-Zionist protestations - was very much a viable box office draw.

> **"** Although the Donmar is a small theatre, it has something epic about it: there is a kind of electricity in there; the fact is, there's no place to hide.
> The auditorium is on three sides but not three equal sides - it's an asymmetrical theatre, which is always difficult. You can't control the audience's perspective because they don't have just one perspective and yet the theatre is not in the round, so it's not an easy space to work in terms of visual theatre. Audiences love the space because they're in the play, really; it's like being on stage or almost like being at a rehearsal. There's a fundamental informality which means that there is no gulf between the audience and the actor and an audience always finds that exciting. Actors find it somewhat unnerving until they get used to it; then they love it. **"**

MATTHEW WARCHUS, director
The Life of Stuff, 1993
True West, 1994

Was twelve years a long enough gap to merit doing the play again? Yes, says Hytner, especially since "neither Sam nor I remembered very much about [Hall's] production." What's more, argued Hytner, who had never previously directed a Williams play, "there was a huge audience that didn't see that production or that saw it that would like to see the play again, particularly with this actress" - namely, Helen Mirren, the Donmar's baleful star. The confines of the theatre meant sacrificing some of the heightened, virtuosic effects that gave Hall's version such an edge. Instead, the aim was to tighten the focus on the play's

essential rapport between Williams' lovesick middle-aged Lady (played by Mirren) and the young guitar-playing Val, a fetching drifter-stud who matches Lady wound for psychic wound. (The play is a rewrite of *Battle of Angels*, Williams' first commercially produced script.) "With epic plays," acknowledges Hytner, "there are losses" to a space like the Donmar - even if, he admits, "the operatic elements of *Orpheus* were something I was happy not to have to deal with." At the same time, says the director, "there are always gains. It did feel as if, done intimately, the intensity between Val and Lady would crackle quite a lot."

And so this *Orpheus* often did, courtesy a sad-eyed Mirren (an Olivier nominee the following year for her performance) and Dublin actor Stuart Townsend, who communicated the poet in Val waiting to be let loose. Inheriting a part played by Marlon Brando on screen in the play's 1959 film adaptation *The Fugitive Kind*, Townsend was a deliberately slighter and freer physical type. "Some of the critics thought

▲ Michael Rudko and Mark Rylance played fratricidal brothers (and swapped roles) in *True West*

Stuart wasn't substantial enough," says Anne McNulty of a part for which the emerging American film star Billy Crudup had initially been considered, "but that was the whole point: Stuart's substance was in his spiritual and not his physical strength." Mirren, meanwhile, blossomed again under Hytner, who had directed her to an Oscar nomination on screen for *The Madness of King George.* Her Lady wasn't the fiery, elemental Italian so fiercely delineated by Redgrave but a quieter, sorrier woman keen for release amid a bigoted redneck environment that damns all Williams' more sensitive souls to hell.

Mirren never saw Redgrave do the part but she had seen Anna Magnani in the film, and that, says Mirren, "was who was hovering in a big way: Anna is my great inspiration as an actress." At the same time, Mirren found *The Fugitive Kind* "also rather a bad film. Strangely, Anna wasn't very good in it, and neither was Marlon Brando: they were both rather wooden." As a result, Mirren says she felt "conscious of the need to reclaim *Orpheus*" amid the "pretty intense" confines of a theatre where she was nightly "tripping over people's feet." Backstage, the star recalls a big cast in period garb all "very very squashed" into the two dressing rooms. "That was pretty intense, and at first, I didn't think I'd be able to handle it. But in the end you couldn't help but become close; it made the experience very strong for all of us."

Mirren isn't sure whether she had ever worked at the Donmar before: "In my mind, I imagine I did, but I don't think that's actually so: my brain is like a sieve." Someone who had was designer Bob Crowley on *Into the Woods* two years previously. On *Orpheus*, Crowley fashioned a floating ceiling like a giant cobweb that became a metaphor for the play, while the proximity of the seating made it seem as if the audience were potential customers in the shop where the play is set. ("It reminded me of one of those shops in west Cork," says Crowley, finding in Williams' damp deep South an unexpected trigger of his own Irish past.) Hytner looks back on the production as "a holiday - the honest truth is there isn't a play in the world that isn't easier to do for two hundred people than one thousand ; if you put a great play with a great actor in front of two hundred people, it's always good, even if you fuck it up" (which he did not). Talking very much from his position as the National Theatre's

> "Like a lot of the small found spaces, the Donmar really works best for the four rows downstairs that sit facing the stage. Those are the people it works best for, though the rest are compensated for by the fact that it still works well because it's small and you're still close to what's going on.
>
> If I were to offer one observation, it's that the enormous success of the Donmar has represented a great shot in the arm to London theatre but in the end is about reintroducing the court theatre to London, and once you join the court, you're in. By virtue of their size, court theatres play to initiates, and anybody can be one: I wouldn't want to suggest at all that it is impossible to be initiated into the courts that are the audiences at the Donmar and at the Almeida, too. My only worry is that if we make ourselves comfortable with the idea that theatre is always best under Donmar circumstances, then gradually theatre makers will lose the appetite for making themselves available to embrace large numbers of people for large numbers of performances.
>
> That said, Sam and Caro have a tremendous set-up - enormously convivial - and Caro is a superb runner of a theatre, superb. Sam has made something very remarkable there."

NICHOLAS HYTNER, director
Orpheus Descending, 2000

artistic director designate, Hytner spoke of it being nearly impossible "not to prefer sitting six feet from Helen Mirren at the Donmar to sitting in the sixth row of the Lyttelton [the National's 900-seat proscenium theatre]. A studio theatre can achieve something close to perfection - close, if you like, to definitive analysis - for the select few who are able to turn up."

With that in mind, it's worth recalling the drama underpinning the Donmar's earlier foray into Williams, Mendes' 1995 revival of *The Glass Menagerie*, the American revival that completed this artistic director's third season. Unlike *Orpheus*, which falls very much into the theatre's economic upswing post-*Blue Room*, *Menagerie* preceded *Company* as a Mendes double-header arriving during that very period when the theatre was threatened with closure. That episode - tense at the time - had a happy ending (see chapter two), and so, aesthetically speaking, did *Glass Menagerie*, which kicked off a Mendes triple through *Company* and *Habeas Corpus* that remains the director's most sustainedly exhilarating sequence of work to date.

As *Company* was an immensely personal project, so was *Glass Menagerie*, a seminal drama about a fractured family coming from a director whose parents had split up when he was three. (Unlike Williams' narrative alter ego Tom, Mendes, however, is an only child.) "I was fascinated partly because of my own relationship to my family: Williams is writing about a mother-son relationship and that sense of entrapment and escape and how that actually fuels creativity and the creative urge." Did Mendes' own father "fall in love with long distance," like the errant telephone man in Williams' play? Not quite. "He pissed off to Plumstead" - though father and son now are remarkably close.

If Mendes had clearly accessed the play's emotions, he was no less clear about how *The Glass Menagerie* should be done. That meant, for starters, casting an unusually young Amanda Wingfield in Zoë Wanamaker, who was in her forties at the time as against the septuagenarian (Jessica Tandy, Constance Cummings) that had become customary in the part. "Amanda still is and has to be sexually current. There's still a sexual undertow to her relationship with her son, still a sexual charge between her and the Gentleman Caller, still a sexual jealousy between her and her daughter, Laura." The point, Mendes went on, is that "Amanda is alive and alert and destroyed by her surroundings and the poverty of her social situation; she's not some stupid old biddy." Rob Howell's design - the first to utilise the upper-level Donmar walkway - had a cage-like feel inhanced by the fire escape surrounding the set, beneath which sat what Mendes thought of as "a real apartment floating in a blue sea of memory." In visual terms, it was a dreamscape tilting over into nightmare. Just like Williams' haunted and haunting play.

Wanamaker thought Mendes "was joking," she says, when he first offered her the role of the bereft chatterbox, Amanda. "I was thrilled but it took me a while to try and get my head around it; I never saw myself as that character." Only once she began her research did Mendes' argument click into place: Wanamaker was pleased to discover that Williams' own mother bore about the same relationship in age to Tennessee as Wanamaker did to the younger members of the cast. Rehearsals were held upstairs at the Old Vic through a sweaty summer during which Wanamaker was losing confidence. "Sometimes, I didn't know where I was going with it, and it was due very much to Sam's cajoling and bullying that I managed

to get there." Wanamaker's colleagues included, as Tom, the rising film actor Ben Chaplin, a 26-year-old who was back in London having spent a year in Los Angeles; Claire Skinner - who would later be Mendes' National Theatre Desdemona - as Laura; and a 22-year-old RADA graduate, Mark Dexter, making his professional stage debut as The Gentleman Caller. "It all happened so quickly," reflects Dexter, "as if I were in a movie."

The production was rife with passions behind the scenes as well as centre stage, not to mention the separate drama accompanying Dexter's diagnosis with measles the day before the first preview - this in a theatre that employs no understudies. (The actor never missed a performance.) Lucy Davies remembers in rehearsals Mendes "really reining in four completely different beasts to play in the same race. They were all very different sorts of performers, and it was a real testimony to Sam's talent as a director that all that was invisible on stage." The friction between the scrupulous Wanamaker and the more freewheeling Chaplin was, says Mendes, "helpful in the end - he was the uncontrollable boy and she was the mother saying, 'This is how it should be; you must obey the rules,' so that was no bad thing." Chaplin still recalls the night when Wanamaker stuck her fingers in her ears during one of his speeches only to have Chaplin pull her hands away from her head so he could bellow the lines right at her. "Zoë was really giving me stuff to work with; there was such a classic mother-son Oedipal thing going on there, and that was bound to affect your relationship. Sometimes, wrongly, she took it personally; sometimes, I took it personally."

If tempers at the time flared - Chaplin admits to having "the theatrical equivalent of Attention Deficit Disorder: I like to mix it up and change it each night" - a legacy of affection remains. "Ben was very sexy," says Wanamaker now. "I'd never seen a Tom like that." To this day, says Chaplin, who had auditioned for a place at London's Guildhall with a scene of Tom's, "I have never been involved in anything where I felt the audience got more from it. *The Glass Menagerie* gives me more pleasure than anything I've done." (The actor lives on for a different reason in Donmar annals for being the person who banned cardboard boxes of Maltesers from the theatre. A good thing, too, Chaplin laughs: "They might as well have handed out raw carrots to the audience.")

The production then moved to the Comedy under the auspices of Thelma Holt, becoming the first Donmar transfer to show a profit in the West End. But Chaplin, ever restless, left it on the Donmar's final

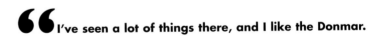

❝❞ I've seen a lot of things there, and I like the Donmar.

night - "a shame," says Wanamaker - and ceded his part to another Ben, i.e. Ben Walden. "It was actually wonderful," says Chaplin, "because I got to go back to see a production I was in." But what the actor never saw was the force field of emotion that he and the Donmar cast generated across the "battleground," says Mendes, that was the Wingfields' flat. The evening's revelations were writ small and large: the punctured "Ohhhh" emanating from Wanamaker's Amanda, a woman no less betrayed than her crippled and indrawn daughter by the Gentleman Caller's belated announcement that he was, in fact, engaged. Dexter, in turn, brought a novel smugness to the late-arriving Jim's bonhomie. How sensitive, after all, is any romantic prospect who can declaim on "the power of love" oblivious to the sight of Skinner's abjectly silent Laura reeling from exactly that?

Chaplin, for his part, had taken his time in rehearsals coming to terms with Tom's celebrated final speech, a requiem for a sister that resonated deeply with the actor, whose own older sister had died of cancer two years earlier, age 33. "I didn't want to do the last speech," says the actor. "It was too emotional, and I was scared. And it was Sam who said, 'You do know it; you know it inside.'" That explains Chaplin's voice on the press night dropping to a hush at the first mention of Laura, his choked delivery of "I tried to leave you behind me" revealing how fully Tom could not. "The play is about escape," Mendes says, "and also a kind of an elegy to a lost life - to a life that Tom has wanted to escape and, now that he's out of it, he wants back again."

The Glass Menagerie more than any Mendes production fed *American Beauty*, another portrait of familial suffocation featuring in Kevin Spacey's Lester Burnham a much older and postmodern variant on Williams' eternally questing Tom: Both Alan Ball's Oscar-winning screenplay and Williams's play work via recollection, while the rose petals so famously deployed in the film made a stage appearance in this production. Alongside *Company*, *Glass Menagerie* awakened Mendes to a more personally revealing choice of projects that would carry over to his work on screen. And at the time, playing to 96% and 100%, respectively, *Menagerie* and *Company* together acted as the best possible advocates for securing the Donmar's future against the funding odds. "I was willing to sit at any table with anyone," says Mendes, "and argue that this theatre does some of the best work in London." But not even the most advanced rhetoric could compare to the argument for survival that is posed by art.

It's a very shapely ship: ship shape.

TOM STOPPARD, playwright
The Real Inspector Hound/Black Comedy
(Warehouse Productions), 1998
The Real Thing, 1999

Donmar 1

ash crisis may pell closure for cclaimed new West End theatr

by ROBIN STRINGER, Arts Correspondent

NE of L
onmar
less it
Both it
elevisio
ort. Ma
2 million
theatre fo

"It is te
We are
uture wit
roducing
ion of spo

"Even p
have been
piecemeal

Evening Standard

Tuesday, 12 September, 1995

The Donmar must be saved

CAN it really be true that the Don... one of London's most ex... atres, is facing...
Despite...

The Arts

30   THURSDAY, 14 SEPTEMBER, 1995

Chained

YOU might think that the arts world is awash with cash. That Richard Eyre at the National Theatre is swimming through crisp £50 notes, that newly minted pound coins are ...London's fringe and that ...layers

---

This is a job for the Arts Cou

The shows sell out. The director (Sam Mendes, *above*) is a star. How can the Donmar be allowed to **David Lister**

sors, Carlton Television, are unwilling to continue funding productions after March. The theatre needs support of £400,000 a year or it will shut down. The artistic director Sam Mendes and administrator Caro Newling do not believe they have a cat in hell's chance of getting £400,000 a year from commercial sponsorship and are now trying to win public funding to stay afloat.

Are there any economics as mad as the economics of theatre? Nine of the Donmar's productions in its three-year life have sold out; but even playing to 85 per cent of ca-out; but even playing to £140,000 sponsorship, break-even

the theatre, onl

It is clearly ti
step in. Mende
don Arts Board
it is unlikely to
believe, a better
see it as a duty
theatre that ha
cesses as *Caba*
It should take
Mendes's tale
a special fund
I would lik
excellence. I
...orth and a

Is there a rich do the Donmar ton

Matt Wolf on Sam Mendes's fight to keep his adventurous theatre open

Sam Mendes, by rights, should be a happy man, and on almost every topic he sounds as if he is. He opens an intriguing ad-hoc American season of work tonight at the Donmar Warehouse with Tennessee Williams's *The Glass Menagerie*, followed in December by an equally anticipated production of Stephen Sondheim's 1970 musical, *Company*.

His West End revival of *Oliver!* is picking theatregoers' pockets with a new Fagin (Jim Dale), even as many view Mendes as a likely successor to Richard Eyre to take over the Royal National Theatre in 1997. In addition, there is his

world, National Lottery money to buy the theatre freehold — the Donmar will shut. What's more, the theatre's sponsorship by Carlton Television (£102,000 a year for three years) ends on December 31 this year.

Stu
Play
loss
alon
awa
rare
ing
dres
revi
latio
pro
and
cen

"I
hav
Aro
two
rare
The

n danger

CASH CRISIS STRIKE
WEST END'S DONM

Mendes directs both pro-

by MATT WOLF

EVENING STANDARD

by red tape

onmar Warehouse needs u
float. Can the arts bureauc
nge? **ALISON ROBERTS**

public perception is, then, a prob-

Mrs V Bottomley MP
House of Commons
LONDON SW1A OAA

107 Sout

Dear Mrs Bottomley

I should like to plead with you for my sanity. My w
theatregoer, has gone into a steep decline since lear
threat of closure of the Donmar.

I have to take her word for it that this is a centre of e
However, what I do know is if you do not rescue this ven
won't be worth living.

I realise that this emotive argument will cut little ice
so lets put it another way.

My wife has worked for the NHS for 25 years with hardly
sickness. However, the trauma which would be caused by th
is likely to effect this good health record. The NHS will
for her absence which in financial terms could amount to
thousand pounds. Then, of course, she will need to seek tre
for depression and I will need counselling to help me cope wi
constant bad temper and nagging. This will be costly to the
Service. In fact the deteriorating domestic situation may
see the breakup of the family unit which is against al
principles of the Conservative Government.

With myself and my wife in this dreadful state of health our
may need to be taken into care, this being a further drain on
welfare state. The dog will become neglected and more public fu
will be required to rehabilitate him into the Battersea Dogs Ho

Surely it would be cheaper in the long run to provide the Don
with some funds.

Yours in trepidation

Mr Jack

More jam for Sam

After an
extraordinary run
of theatrical
successes,
director Sam
Mendes is about to
take on his biggest
challenge yet.
He talks to
Charles Spencer

Men
Lond
re
un
a
ri
l
ov
op

T
ec
le
len
ma
var
cle
tal
is

Th
m

FORTUNE seems to
smile on the young
director Sam Mendes.
Since he left Cambridge in
1987 (he got a first, naturally), his career has been a
continuous arc of success.
Now, at 27, he has been given

DONMAR

i'm a believer

first revivals find a
home at the
donmar

chapter 5

What do you do after you've reclaimed Tennessee Williams and Stephen Sondheim? Sam Mendes' answer in 1996 was to swing the programming pendulum about as firmly back to Britain as it was possible to go. After all, it's not every Donmar show that has Stevenage as a punch line.

An appeal to the Hertfordshire theatregoer wasn't the only reason, of course, to mount the first professional London revival of *Habeas Corpus*, Alan Bennett's 1973 play. Well into his fourth season, Mendes was noting trends to Donmar attendance patterns that needed to be reflected in the repertoire. Produce an untried play, no matter how well-known the author, and the audience seemed not to want to know: the Mendes regime's tyro production, Athol Fugard's highly regarded *Playland*, had played to a dispiriting 44%. Sometimes, reviews were to blame: few leapt for tickets in the Donmar's first season to Michael Frayn's *Here*, which fell during that dramatist's creative dip stretching from *Benefactors* in 1984 through to *Copenhagen* fourteen years on. But even well-reviewed new plays (*The Life of Stuff*, for instance, which followed *Here* directly into the Donmar) were playing to far less than half the attendance of *Translations* or *Design For Living* in the first and second seasons.

The apparent lesson: for a theatre that at the time was still finding its footing while remaining committed to short runs, it simply wasn't possible to build up a head of steam around most new scripts. (*The Blue Room* would assist in changing matters.) It's no accident that Mendes' choice of original projects came with names like Stephen Sondheim and Nicole Kidman attached. Only late in his tenure and once he had won his Oscar - when, in other words, Mendes' own name was the self-evident draw - could the director again gamble Donmar resources on an entirely unknown writer: very successfully so in the case of Nick Whitby's *To the Green Fields Beyond*.

At the same time, one could scarcely feel too upset about being thrown back on an existing canon that allowed Alan Bennett and, before him, Brian Friel to be revealed anew. "*The Life of Stuff* killed us; we loved it, but we shot our foot off doing it," acknowledges Mendes, who came upon a solution that would emerge as unwritten policy. "We soon saw the value in picking great plays with one previous production in the 1980s or late 70s and rediscovering them" - a reborn studio theatre conferring its own values and strengths on an extant text.

His first such Donmar foray was *Translations*, a play Mendes had previously directed early in his days at Chichester. But he felt no qualms about returning to Brian Friel's exquisitely layered play twelve years after its Hampstead Theatre debut in London had warranted a transfer to the National. Mendes first saw

◄ Jim Broadbent

the play in a university production during his time at Cambridge (that go-round was designed by his friend and fellow student Tom Piper, who would later come to design for the Donmar) and had found it "one of the saddest and most beautiful and most delicate things I had ever seen - a play that was truly romantic and truly political at the same time." And because he had directed *Translations* five years before, Mendes felt confident about "stripping it bare scenically"; Johan Engels' design - an enormous tree alongside some stools and a small pile of books - is among the Donmar's simplest and most easily read, so to speak, to date. In physical terms, the challenge posed by the production had to do with keeping dust levels low on a stage filled with drying peat: a spray made up of water mixed with glycerine did the trick.

Set in 1833 at a so-called "hedge-school" in rural Ireland, the play maps out Friel's usual County Donegal landscape at a historically decisive time: that period of map-making when place names in Irish-speaking communities like Baile Beag were being rendered into their English equivalents, i.e. Ballybeg. On one level, *Translations* is a richly allusive meditation on tribal behaviour and cultural usurpation that comes steeped in quotations from the classics. (The Times' Benedict Nightingale has wonderfully characterised Friel's text as "thinky.") And yet, at *Translations*' bursting heart lies a love scene of enduring power between Yolland, an English lieutenant new to the region, and an Irish villager called Maire. Neither can speak the other's language, which shouldn't matter in an environment where local villager Doalty is himself learning the verb, "conjugo, I join together." But it is a wise author's quietly blistering point - the play, one must not forget, was written in 1980 to launch Friel and Stephen Rea's politically pro-active company Field Day - that a people and its land can so easily be torn apart. That explained the power of a climactic scenic coup devised by Mendes to rival his far more overtly shocking conclusion to *Cabaret*. While the schoolmaster Hugh was delivering the closing speech about his own country's road to ruin, an illuminated outline of a map of Ireland came slowly into view. "In a play about the tussle over an island," says Mendes, "I wanted - without hitting the audience over the head - to remind them that the issue has not yet been resolved."

The moment, visceral and yet poignantly evocative, showed how a director working boldly on the front foot in *Assassins* and *Cabaret* could step imaginatively back, as well: whereas *Cabaret* always felt like a high-concept directorial take on the work, *Translations* worked subtly - and mournfully - outward from the text. Mendes found doing the play again "much more enjoyable" than the first time around "because I didn't feel I was learning about the play at the same time as the actors." Donmar general manager Nick Frankfort was the Friel revival's company manager. "For me," he says, *Translations* "remains quintessential Sam - clear storytelling combined with poetry and getting fantastic performances out of quite different performers." Playing the schoolteacher's elder son was Finbar Lynch (at the time going by the name Barry), who felt the cricket skills of his director at work on Friel's play. "Sam is very at home in a team situation, which is what we had in *Translations*; there were no big egos." As for a venue to which the actor would return twice in the next seven years, "I remember at the first preview of *Translations* feeling like I was on a mantlepiece; it seemed like there was nowhere to hide." Which only amplified the impact of one of Mendes' two finest directorial achievements never to move or be seen elsewhere.

That wasn't for lack of trying: news of *Translations*' London success at the Donmar spread to New York, where producers did their best to interest him in remounting the play there. "I had just finished *Oliver!* and was too exhausted," says Mendes, who in any case wanted "a much more intimate" production of the play than most Broadway venues would allow. Instead, *Translations* ended up briefly at

Finbar Lynch in *Translations* ▶

the Plymouth Theatre directed by Howard Davies and starring Brian Dennehy and Rufus Sewell before doing a fast fade. "Having seen it, I kicked myself," says Mendes, in hindsight regretting his hesitation to do the play again himself. But by that point the director was already moving on to Alan Bennett's farce - a putative English seaside postcard of a play that turned out to be amazingly alive with feeling. In time, *Habeas Corpus*, like *Translations*, would also be discussed at length for possible transfers to both the West End and New York that also never happened. (Miriam Margolyes even faxed the Donmar from Los Angeles to put herself forward personally for any follow-up production of the play: "I know it's bad form to bother you directly, but I'd go anywhere at the drop of a pair of knickers.") But a further life at the Aldwych Theatre was not to be, to the distress of Margolyes and others. Only those who caught the play during its 1996 summer run at the Donmar saw this director at his most accomplished.

Mendes was well aware of the contrast between *Habeas Corpus* and the double he had just completed with *Glass Menagerie* and *Company*. "I'd done these two American plays and suddenly here was this very very English play suffused with the spirit of *Carry On* movies and yet deeply expressive of the English malaise - and the need to be desired." At first, Bennett wasn't entirely sure he wanted a fresh outing for a play featuring a community of people for whom sex is life only to end with its central figure, a salaciously inclined Sussex GP, doing a dance of death. The playwright had already refused an earlier request from Richard Eyre to revive *Habeas Corpus* at the National - "simply," Bennett says, "because it was so perfectly done the first time around; that's what had stuck in the mind, and I wanted to remember it as it was." True, he had at one point permitted RADA to do a student production of the script, utilising the actual prompt books from the original West End staging of a different Eyre, namely Ronald. (Jane Horrocks and Imogen Stubbs were in the RADA cast.) The Donmar, however, was a different animal altogether, and time had moved on, says Bennett, who admits to "being overprotective of [*Habeas Corpus*]." Bennett sanctioned the play on one condition - that Mendes steer clear of the literal-mindedness and clutter that had swamped the play in 1976 on Broadway, where the company had included (of all unlikely castmates) Donald Sinden and Richard Gere.

Hardly a Donmar production has been more luxuriantly cast in depth. Jim Broadbent - still in his pre-Oscar days - was happy to inherit the Sinden-Alec Guinness role as Dr. Wicksteed, the sex-obsessed doctor. "I'd done lots of small intimate theatres over the years," says the actor of the play's initial appeal, "and a lot of Alan Bennett. He and Sam seemed a good combination, and it was a relatively short run. The whole thing was good." Playing his wife was another performer, Brenda Blethyn, who would come to the attention of the Academy Awards even sooner. It was during a *Habeas Corpus* run-through one May morning that the actress got called away to the Cannes Festival for twenty-four hours to collect her acting prize for the film *Secrets and Lies*. "Brenda screamed and fell to her knees," says Mendes, who was at rehearsals to witness Blethyn's reaction to news of her win. "The next day she came back from Cannes with her scroll." The high level of casting carried through to, among others, Jason Watkins, Sarah Woodward, Celia Imrie, and Imelda Staunton, the last-named making her Donmar debut in a role once played by Bennett: the obsessive cleaner, Mrs. Swabb. (Her refrain: "hoover hoover hoover.") Playing the deliciously named Canon Throbbing was Hugh Bonneville, who would later play a younger Jim Broadbent in the film of *Iris*.

In performance, the sense of ensemble seemed effortless but took time to achieve. "Sam said it was the most difficult play he had ever directed," says Staunton, "and it was certainly difficult to grasp for all of us, I think." So unsure was she that at one point Staunton thought of bailing out, "and that had never happened to me before." One exchange between the actress and her director seems especially amusing in retrospect, given the joyful sellout that the show became. Reports Staunton: "Sam said to me, 'You're not doing anything with the part,' and I said to him, 'Well, you're not being any bloody help.'" From there, she adds, "cut to: I have never laughed so much in a rehearsal room; suddenly, it all clicked." And just as suddenly Staunton was away, sporting for the part a headscarf with her hair in a roller in the front, socks rolled down to the ankle.

Habeas Corpus was seen the first time around in a Shaftesbury Avenue proscenium house, the Lyric, but Bennett's scripted request for an open and minimally furnished stage turned out to suit the Donmar. What's more, there was little danger of Rob Howell's cloud-filled set - the self-evident influence was Magritte - getting in the way of the text's elegant swing between uproariously rude comedy and a pathos that cut like a knife. As directed by Mendes, Bennett's text echoed Alan Ayckbourn in high-embarrassment mode one minute, Ortonesque subversion the next, as befits a script that marches to a distinctly alliterative mantle: Dr. Wicksteed's "he whose lust lasts, lasts longest." The production may have been tough in rehearsals on the actors in the way that comedies often are ("people stop laughing," says Mendes, "after about three days and it suddenly becomes a very, very precise technical job that can get very gruelling") but the payoff came in performance. In the end, Bennett wasn't the only one who "thought it was terrific," even if he did find himself missing the gains to be had in a larger proscenium theatre that come with "lines," Bennett says, "that are so outrageous that they need to go to the back wall and then come back." Among those clamouring for tickets one night was a latecomer who was more than

Designer Rob Howell's intentionally bare set for *Habeas Corpus* ▲

happy to stand and watch the first act from the rear of the circle. Afterwards, he made a point of thanking theatre manager Julia Christie and box office manager Barry Ashby. The theatregoer's name: Tony Blair, who several years later had clearly learned his lesson. When he and Cherie came to the Donmar together in 1998 to see *The Blue Room*, the couple were on time.

A no less interesting side show to *Habeas'* onstage shenanigans occurred between performances on matinee days in the theatre's upstairs bar. Twice a week between the two Thursday and Saturday shows, the *Habeas* cast would get dolled up for a series of non-alcoholic parties in which they all pretended to be aboard a ship. (The vaguely nautical curve to the circle bar no doubt enhanced credibility.) The idea, Imelda Staunton remembers, was that the cast was on a 72-month cruise, "and I would do things over the microphone like, 'There will be drinks on poop deck.' It was a very, very intense forty minutes." The *Habeas* ensemble was "the maddest cast," theatre manager Julia Christie recalls with affection, not least because the Donmar front-of-house staff got to join in the antics. That they could be flexible, as well, was borne out one night when company member Stewart Permutt,

playing the small role of the ailing Mr. Purdue, became ill himself and couldn't go on. What to do? After some quick re-rehearsal, which neatly dispensed with the need for Permutt actually to appear on stage, Mendes decided against identifying for the public precisely which cast member was unwell; instead, he wanted to see if anyone would notice or be put out. Before the show, Mendes told that night's audience that there was one actor off ill but that the touch-up rehearsals should have smoothed over any cracks - though the theatre would, of course, offer refunds should people want them. "And, of course," says Christie, "because it was from Sam and he was saying, 'I've re-directed it,' they all loved it." (No one requested money back.) It was during the technical week prior to public performances of *Habeas Corpus* that Lucy Ryan joined the Donmar as general assistant, though she would move on over four years to the

▲ The cast of *Habeas Corpus* cuts up for the camera

job of marketing coordinator. "It was a great time to start," says Ryan. "I thought it can't get any better than this." She laughs. "That's the strength of the Donmar: there's always a great production around the corner. And they still keep coming."

From *Habeas Corpus* on, the revelatory revivals started arriving thick and fast, plucked almost entirely from the recent past alongside one 2,400-year-old play, Sophocles' *Electra*, that had an unexpected currency and force. It's no surprise in the theatre's chronology of its own work - a listing that finds revivals over the Mendes decade outnumbering new work by more than two to one - that Frank McGuinness' unsparing version of a time-honoured text should be classified as a "world premiere": not only did the Donmar commission the script, going on to mount it first at Chichester prior to London in a co-production with Duncan Weldon, but the same production's remarkable eventual success on Broadway bore testament to what one might call the shock of the old. In theory, the inclusion of so ages-old a play in a theatre that had generally steered itself toward a twentieth-century bias might have seemed out of place. But as directed by David Leveaux and performed with feral commitment by Zoë Wanamaker, *Electra* emerged as a play for now - whether or not one was aware of the grave-side image of a Bosnian girl, no more than eleven or twelve, that helped fuel Leveaux's desire to do the play.

As she had felt at first toward *The Glass Menagerie*'s Amanda, Zoë Wanamaker was no more sure about taking on Electra, a role Fiona Shaw had not long before played for director Deborah Warner in a take-no-prisoners aria of grief. "I felt it had been done," says Wanamaker, "and I didn't feel I was capable of doing it." Duncan Weldon was pitching *Eccentricities of A Nightingale* in an effort to push the actress still further down the Tennessee Williams path. But when Leveaux over lunch countered by offering *Electra*, Wanamaker had to decide: "I'd never thought of that and had never connected myself with big drama, which is Greek drama; I had always shied away from the Greek stuff." Leveaux, in turn, would be tackling the play for the second time in three years, having done a different translation of *Electra* in Tokyo in 1995 with a local actress, Sato Orie, in the title role.

At the Donmar, Wanamaker gave a flintier account of Sophocles' anguished heroine than Fiona Shaw had in 1988: whereas Shaw offered one long suppurating howl of pain, an envenomed Wanamaker stalked the palace in her murdered father's ill-fitting and threadbare coat - the rampaging adult at distinct odds with the poignantly innocent picture of Wanamaker as a child that appeared on the cover of the poster and the published text. (No other Donmar production has used for marketing purposes a childhood still of its star.) *Electra* is exactly the sort of play where one might expect the Donmar's communal dressing rooms to irritate those performers in need of privacy and calm. Not at all, according to Jenny Galloway, who was in superb form yet again at this address, here playing the matter-of-fact Chorus of Mycenae. "You would have thought somebody playing Electra would want to have a bit of a quiet time." Instead, Galloway gave Wanamaker a recording of "Don't Rain On My Parade" from *Funny Girl* and "whenever Zoë was having a particularly hard time, there'd be a quick blast of the song and on she would go."

Not that concentration - from the audience as well as the actors - wasn't essential during the show. One Thursday matinee made news when Wanamaker broke the fourth wall to tell off a noisy gathering of French schoolchildren. "If Zoë hadn't done it, I would have," says Galloway, who was mid-scene with Wanamaker at the time. "When you're delivering the text of *Electra* to somebody four feet away and they're being disruptive, you either go over and hit them - or you tell them off." Though the tabloid press tried to play up the episode as some kind of international incident (the English having a go at the

French), "nobody came to complain," says Julia Christie. "The audience was, like, 'Good for Zoë.'" About the only person who didn't respond to the performance was an ageing actor who had been made homeless and whom Christie remembers making a nuisance of himself in the foyer. "He used to walk in and point at the pictures of Zoë and shout, 'Rubbish! She can't do this! How dare she?'" His, needless to say, was the minority opinion.

The star's journey with the play wasn't finished yet, even if winning both a Variety Club Best Actress award and an Olivier still failed to persuade her to undertake a West End transfer. Wanamaker had her sights set on reprising *Electra* on Broadway, where the New York-born actress had been well-reviewed twice before. (And received Tony nominations both times, for *Piaf* and then for *Loot*.) *Electra*, then, was

> **The Donmar is almost like an informal space: it's not intimidating at all, and it's certainly not sophisticated backstage. But the whole thing about it is upbeat: even if you're playing something downbeat, the experience is upbeat. There's no trickery there, just artistry - does that make sense? It sounds terribly phony.**
>
> **BRENDA BLETHYN**, actress
> Habeas Corpus, 1996

her chance to headline an American company in a play that she was finding valuably cathartic. "You're not supposed to use theatre as your psychological casting couch," says Wanamaker, who had lost both her parents by then, "but I'm afraid that's what happens to us as actors: we're walking vessels, really. David had asked me if I'd like to do it, telling me I needed a good scream. And he was right." And so she signed with Leveaux to do the play again a year later, this time with a different supporting cast headed by the scaldingly elegant Clytemnestra of Claire Bloom. The production sold out a three-week early-autumn run in 1998 at the McCarter Theatre on the Princeton campus and got raves, a real money notice from New York Times then-deputy theatre critic Peter Marks included; by December, it had opened on Broadway.

Ensconced in the very dressing room occupied fifty years earlier by Marlon Brando in *A Streetcar Named Desire*, Wanamaker found herself premiering the same week as - and two streets away from - Nicole Kidman in *The Blue Room*: two "Donmarines," in Caro Newling's choice word, busily doing up Manhattan. And though that turned out to be a busy autumn for the Greeks in Manhattan - Medea, Iphigenia, and Oedipus were all getting a look-in on other stages around town - Sophocles' traumatised heroine more than held her own. The *Electra* engagement was extended to well beyond double its eight-week run, by the end of which Wanamaker found herself exhausted but elated, too. (Interestingly, although illness forced her to miss several performances of the play in London, she was never off once in New York.) "I got terrible eczema, lost weight, my back was bad" - indeed, so shorn and mutilated was her hair for the part that a fellow gallery-goer at the Museum of Modern Art one day advised folic acid as a remedy. But free of all vanity, the actress knew her fearlessness had triumphed. "*Electra* was an event," says Wanamaker, "and that was what we always wanted it to be."

If familial devastation was raised in *Electra* to a literally murderous pitch, two subsequent Donmar revivals exposed the bruises left by the *Habeas Corpus* GP Wicksteed's favourite topic, lust. Peter Nichols' *Passion Play* had two separate outings the first time round, first at the Aldwych in 1981 and then at Wyndham's, in addition to a short-lived Broadway version, starring Frank Langella, that got produced in 1983 under the single word *Passion* - not to be confused with the 1994 musical of the same name by Nichols' chum, Stephen Sondheim. ("It was a terrible disaster," Nichols says of his own play's Broadway premiere. "I kind of gave way to pressure; the producer literally threw it on.") Its London debut had brought *Passion Play* an Evening Standard Drama Award, and Nichols was keen for a revival. "Anyone who wants to do any of my stuff can do it anywhere. It's always nice to be done and to be resuscitated with the kiss of life." Nichols pauses before adding the stinger. "It would be nicer still if people did some of my new plays."

Nichols had never previously worked with the revival's director, Michael Grandage, but the playwright was emboldened by his happy collaborations over time with directors of that name: Michael Blakemore, who first staged *A Day in the Death of Joe Egg*, and the late Mike Ockrent, who had done that Royal Shakespeare Company premiere of *Passion Play*. It helped that Nichols remembered the Donmar fondly from its Warehouse days, having seen *Educating Rita* there as well as the McKellen-Dench *Macbeth*. As an environment, says Nichols, "the Donmar exposes the play, and that's what audiences seem to like." Even by its own standards, however, the theatre has scarcely seen as scalpel-sharp an account of the ravages of desire as *Passion Play* got from Grandage and his cast, among whom the sight of an increasingly ashen Cherie Lunghi - playing a woman whose husband of twenty-five years has fallen for a much-younger woman - lives on bruisingly in the memory.

"It was entirely about what we created in that very tiny auditorium in terms of it being almost unbearable to watch," says Grandage, who quickly dispensed with Nichols' scripted set requirements in an attempt to create a mostly unadorned and elemental space. While *The Glass Menagerie* and *Company* had made a point of specifically using the Donmar's upper gantry, *Passion Play* chose not to - an ironic decision given that Nichols' play is very intentionally written to be performed on two levels. "When Michael told me there would be no upstairs, I was deeply shocked," says Nichols. "It had worked so well in *Company* that I had assumed it was something he would use." Instead, it was as if designer Christopher Oram wanted as little as possible to get in the way of the breadth of feeling of the play. Gone were the revolves and the four (at least) separate playing areas called for in the script in favour of a single sofa as the visual focus. The production, says Nichols, "cut out every bit of extraneous scenery, which I thought was very brave."

Equally bold was the prevailing bleakness of an ironically titled evening (Nichols' true topic is the extinction of passion) that tended to divide people along gender lines. His authorial conceit - familiar from, among other plays, Brian Friel's *Philadelphia, Here I Come!* - was to dramatise what might be called the bifurcated self, so that both the philandering James and his wronged wife, Eleanor, have alter egos, Jim and Nell, that shadow them throughout the play. But not every female spectator in 2000 was willing to buy into Eleanor/Nell's apparent willingness to wilt, when many woman in the same situation nowadays would show James/Jim the door. On the other hand, writing not for the first time from personal experience, Nichols was being true to the facts of his own life - with Grandage reporting the

> **"People's loyalty and love of the theatre rub off on you, and as far as the acting is concerned, there's never any sense that 'you're the next lot in'; not at all. Everyone has all worked there for a long time, so obviously it does feel like a family - and you're embraced. The Donmar is such an extraordinary place: the thing is, it seems the biggest theatre in England in many respects."**
>
> **IMELDA STAUNTON**, actress
> Habeas Corpus, 1996
> Divas at the Donmar, 1998

sense of alarm that he as a director felt on that particular night when Nichols announced that the real-life inspiration for Kate (the younger woman) would be in to see the show. For himself, Grandage wanted to make the point by the end of the play that "walking out sometimes is not a solution" - as the director saw for himself on the first night. "There Peter and Thelma [Nichols] were on opening night sitting next to each other," says Grandage, clearly moved by the memory: "Peter being very proud of what he had achieved and Thelma sharing in it."

If Grandage's Donmar inaugural with C. P. Taylor's *Good* the season before had made for an oddly blank and characterless evening (its chief strength was Oram's stunningly clean-lined, geometric set), *Passion Play* fully bore out Nichols' sense of the Donmar as an "operating theatre" that had cut open something bleakly resonant in a nineteen-year-old play. The production went on to transfer to the Comedy Theatre - Nicky Henson replaced Martin Jarvis as Jim, a substitution Nichols says he preferred - where it made for unlikely summer fare. (Uncommercial, too: the show closed two weeks early, after ten weeks instead of twelve.) As for New York, Nichols turned out to be twice unlucky with this play. A victim of his own unfortunate timing, Nichols - "short of dough," he says, "and waiting for something to happen" - had given away *Passion Play*'s American rights prior to the Donmar opening so that by the time the London version was receiving all due acclaim, a separate Off-Broadway production was already in the works. Its director was Elinor Renfield, a one-time actress who made a point of seeing the Grandage staging several times. To little avail: her production came and went at the Minetta Lane Theatre in Greenwich Village nearly as quickly as its Broadway predecessor had all those years before. Perhaps Nichols ought at some point to try again. Doubtful, he says wryly: "two flops is stretching it quite a bit."

> I like the Donmar very much as a space - it's very interesting and good. I can't quite see why it works so well, though it does, and why such a variety of things seem to work there. I suppose it's to do with an audience used through TV and film to being close, but it's amazing that they can do such big productions: *Company* and *The Front Page* and *Privates On Parade*.
> If I had to criticise the Donmar, there's a sort of snobbery about them, a kind of elitism - and I'm all for elitisms, I'm all for elites - which says, 'You come to us.' It's an exclusive attitude, I think.

PETER NICHOLS, playwright
Passion Play, 2000
Privates On Parade, 2001

Two hits, meanwhile, might be asking rather a lot. But that was the happy fate on both sides of the Atlantic of the Donmar's first revival of another seminal play about adultery, Tom Stoppard's *The Real Thing*. First produced the season after the original *Passion Play*, Stoppard's play had a long and successful West End season at the Strand, where it was directed by Peter Wood, and an even more extravagantly successful run on Broadway in a high-adrenaline and glamorous production from Mike Nichols. What, then, could the Donmar hope to offer the same play? Easy: Stephen Dillane, whose performance as the cuckolded playwright Henry showed the way in which imploding on stage can make a lasting impact. "I remember a phone conversation," says David Leveaux, who directed the revival, "where Stephen said to me, 'What can we bring to this play that's new?' And I said, 'You.'"

Playwright Peter Nichols, author of *Passion Play* and (with Denis King) *Privates On Parade* ▶

> It's a very demanding space and can be a quite hard one in which to time comedy because you can't always hit the whole audience at the same time, even though you feel in such a small space, you should be able to. You can see the whites of the audience's eyes, so you have to be entirely truthful at all times. Just the fact that you can see who's in the front row is kind of defining; there can be a whole house full of people whose faces you recognise.
> I remember seeing *Company*, which I liked a lot, and *The Glass Menagerie*, which I didn't like so much. But it's just one of those places, like the Young Vic, where it's always worth seeing what's on.
> You do get very familiar with Caro and Anne and get to know who's around. It was very nice to go back for a second play having done the first one and having the feeling that you were part of this club of people who were welcome at the Donmar.

STEPHEN DILLANE, actor
Endgame, 1996
The Real Thing, 1999

The actor had been at the Donmar four seasons before, playing Clov to Alun Armstrong's Hamm in a revival of *Endgame*, directed by Katie Mitchell, which wasn't enormous fun either offstage or on. But Stoppard and Leveaux both had an idea that Dillane's inbuilt restraint might bring something rather startling to the potentially showy role of Henry, which had won a Tony Award for Jeremy Irons in New York in what remains one of the most-laureled of all Broadway plays. (The production won five 1984 Tonys, including best play.) Sixteen years later, says Anne McNulty, "Tom [Stoppard] felt duty-bound to make sure Stephen knew just how important he felt it was for Stephen to do the role and for Stephen to know that Tom felt he should do the role; at one point, I think Tom was considering the possibility of ballooning into Stephen's garden."

Stoppard had seen the actor's West End *Hamlet* for Peter Hall in 1994, as well as some earlier work for Peter Wood in a National Theatre revival of *The Beaux' Stratagem*. (That was during the period that Dillane was for Equity reasons acting under the surname Dillon.) "I hadn't seen a lot of Stephen," says Stoppard, "but I just knew he was a special actor," with a selectivity toward work that bode well for *The Real Thing*. "Stephen's a very choosy actor, as he ought to be, so when he said he wanted to do [the Donmar run], it perked me up about the play itself; it was a nice thing to happen before we had even begun, since Stephen is not someone who's glad to get the job." The Donmar itself played a major role in Dillane taking on the play. "I'm not sure I'd have accepted it," says the actor, "if the production had been *The Real Thing* in the West End: there's an image that the Donmar has which makes you think the work is going to be of a certain quality and a certain attitude and attract a certain audience."

First, though, was the need to find a leading lady for Dillane - someone to play Annie, the actress and

▲ Anita Waxman, co-producer of the Donmar's *The Real Thing* in New York, gives Sam Mendes a hug at its Broadway opening in April 2000

free spirit who makes a cuckold out of her rhetorically gifted and suavely spoken playwright-husband, Henry. Emma Fielding, the extraordinary Thomasina in the National Theatre premiere of Stoppard's *Arcadia*, thought about the role but plumped for a National revival of *Look Back In Anger* instead. That left the way clear for her first appearance at the Donmar of Jennifer Ehle, a young performer (29 when the production opened, she was thirteen years Dillane's junior) who had become a star off the back of playing Elizabeth Bennet in *Pride and Prejudice* for BBC-TV. As a teenager, Ehle had in fact seen *The Real Thing* on Broadway since her mother, Rosemary Harris, had been appearing next door in the New York premiere of Hugh Whitemore's *Pack of Lies*. As luck would have it, Ehle caught the final performance of the original Broadway Annie, Glenn Close, and quickly became, she says, "a bit obsessed by the play." Annie is arguably the trickier of the play's two leading roles, since it is left to her to communicate via sheer presence what Henry - who fields a show-stopping second-act speech about language invoking a cricket bat to abet his cause - can let fly with words. Stoppard was thrilled to get Ehle, who by her own admission had been sitting idle and out of work in London for nine months when the offer came. With Ehle, says the playwright, "you feel you're watching somebody living and suffering there, but you see her through a slight swirl of deception, and she's got the most wonderful face and eyes - like somebody who stopped crying an hour ago."

Leveaux had in fact been in New York in 1984 directing a separate version for Broadway of his Riverside Studios production of *A Moon For the Misbegotten*, so he, like Ehle, had seen the Mike Nichols production of *The Real Thing* to which the Donmar staging would pose a striking counterpoint. (Indeed, Leveaux lost the best director Tony that year to Mike Nichols.) "I recall the sheer speed," Leveaux says of Nichols' Broadway approach to the play, which had combined a technical virtuosity - Tony Walton's turntable sets seemed to whip in and out of view - with a sustained high-style bravura in performance. "That production was ruthlessly well managed." But whereas Nichols had told Leveaux that "the vital thing about *The Real Thing* is to find a way of making the scene changes go quickly," the younger director did not agree: "It didn't seem inevitable to me that you had to do the play that way. To the extent that we could be, as it were, anti-Broadway by not taking Mike's solution, we were able to unlock beats that could not be present for Mike."

The result was what Stoppard referred to as a "deconstructed" version of his play - "as if I knew what the word means." Vicki Mortimer's almost modular set established a prevailing interest in the abiding emotional truths of the play, not the trappings of it, which in turn gave a different hue to Stoppard's verbal dexterity. "Tom doesn't write for reasons of flash," says Leveaux. "His writing is not actually flashy, although it can seem like that; it's based in a natural reality." Reviving a play long heralded as the one in which a wizard of wordplay at last showed some heart, Leveaux was conscious of

Playwright Tom Stoppard in rehearsal for *The Real Thing* ▲

deglamourising the play somewhat: playing Henry's first wife, a crisp and close-cropped Sarah Woodward cut far less of a fashion plate than the Tony-winning Christine Baranski had done in New York. At least one of the songs woven into Stoppard's text ended up being different, as well, with the Walker Brothers' "The Sun Ain't Gonna Shine Anymore" after sixteen performances at the Donmar replacing "You've Lost That Loving Feeling" for reasons to do with obtaining the rights. Stoppard was disappointed, speaking as the person who, he says, "had disinterred" the Righteous Brothers' classic all those years before. Nonetheless, the trading off of one pop standard for another aside, the core remained to a play that, says Leveaux, "I had always thought was Tom's memo to himself about the limitations of language" - about a reveller in words, Henry, who is forced to confront that less easily controlled frontier beyond epigrammatic finesse that has to do with feeling.

▲ Jennifer Ehle in *The Real Thing*

STEPPING INTO FREEDOM

The production took its cue from the casual melancholy projected by Dillane, in conjunction with an utterly unforced and rumpled charm that together created a seminal Donmar performance - and one from which Mendes, busy doing his Oscar-related duties on *American Beauty*, was more or less absent. (On that front, he further credits Caro Newling for her careful nurturing of a project that Mendes calls "one of the two or three best things we've done in ten years.") Among Dillane's admirers was Nicole Kidman, who would later play Virginia Woolf opposite the actor's Leonard Woolf in the film *The Hours*. "I saw *The Real Thing* with Sam and we just looked at each other and went, 'We've just seen one of the greatest theatre performances of all time.' It was so present and alive and truthful - there was no pretence or performance." That very asset came to bedevil the production

> **"It just seemed impossibly cool for somebody like me to be involved in something at the Donmar. I had seen *Nine* there and knew that the theatre had that thing about it - that sheen and also the glamour of the Nicole Kidman play that had caused a stir.**
>
> **Somehow the place just works, and you forgive it any problems that there are because that's part of what makes the whole experience just special. I think its imperfections help with the intimacy, although the whole thing only works because so often the plays are so good.**
>
> **You know at the Donmar when you agree to do the play that you are getting paid 200-odd quid a week. And still you're gagging to go, gagging to do it."**
>
> **JENNIFER EHLE**, actress
> The Real Thing, 1999

somewhat during its immensely profitable West End transfer to the Albery early in 2000. (The engagement earned the Donmar £100,000 over ten weeks.) The shift away from the Donmar's close quarters to a proscenium-arch house wasn't being matched with the needed lift in volume and scale of performance from Dillane, whose minutely detailed work risked disappearing across the footlights. The very first Albery performance was interrupted by shouts from the audience to the stage demanding that Dillane speak up. "Mr. Dillane coped admirably," reads that evening's show report, "and then brought up levels." At the time, Dillane spoke to me of his take on the problem. "The trouble with these big theatres is you go in and sit down, and you're immediately alienated by someone booming at you when I'm more interested in getting out of the way of the story."

But it wasn't until that spring when it reached Broadway's Barrymore Theatre, the home two seasons earlier to Leveaux's *Electra*, that *The Real Thing* rediscovered what had distinguished the production at the Donmar, this time pushed up a notch. Before that, says Stoppard, the issue was "the usual Donmar transfer problem: at the Donmar, the audience can eavesdrop, and at a regular theatre, the stuff has got to be pitched at them." Leveaux cites a hard-line resistance to "the virtuoso turn" from both Ehle and Dillane: "The dilemma was to persuade two reactive actors that it was all right and not inherently false to be proactive." He impressed upon the company "the need to step over the line completely: you can't make a certain kind of truthfulness simply louder; what you have to do is accept that the whole plane needs to alter because there's another kind of truth. A bigger pitch can still bring with it the possibility of complexity and speed." As Mendes describes the problem: "Stephen is absolutely obsessively truthful, but stage truth and truth are sometimes two different things."

The Leveaux pep talk worked, and so did float mikes facilitating the acoustics in the Broadway house. The production, says Ehle, "probably was very close to how it was at the beginning by the end; they say you spend the whole time getting back to the read through." Whatever the reason, the show's creators had retrieved in New York what went missing somewhat on the West End. Praising "a sensual sparkle that was less evident" with the same play in 1984, Ben Brantley in The New York Times led a near-uniform set of raves. And in its penultimate week, *The Real Thing* paid back production costs of $1.7 million without being the take-the-town standing room only occasion that the Irons-Close version had been two decades

> " William Gaskill said of the Royal Court that your policy is the people you work with, and that is completely borne out by my experience of the Donmar: It's a genuinely frontline theatre made out of the people who are there. With Sam, it always comes down to casting; he just casts brilliantly - he cast Caro and he cast Anne, and what a blinding piece of casting that was.
> What happens is you go into the Donmar to do a show and they are so entirely consumed with your show that you never feel there's a hierarchy - that some shows are more significant than others; from the start, I immediately just felt, this is like home.
> *Nine* came at a time when I'd been more particularly not here than usual, and I think I felt, well, if one is going to work in England, it's better to work in a place that's kind of home. What I have loved about the Donmar is the group of people one works with there, but if you separate that from the physical space, I've never found the physical space as exciting as some other spaces. On the other hand, it does allow a fantastic, privileged intimacy; that is something very special. "

DAVID LEVEAUX, director
Nine, 1996
Electra, 1997
The Real Thing, 1999

previously. (For one thing, unlike the Mike Nichols production, which over time fielded various replacement casts, a decision was taken not to replace Dillane, Ehle, and co., even though names like Mick Jagger and Gwyneth Paltrow were optimistically - some might argue foolishly - put forward.) The Donmar, once again under Rachel Weinstein's savvy eye, raised £105,000 from an April 5 gala benefit performance: the theatre's most lucrative New York fundraiser yet.

The Brantley review had called Dillane "immensely appealing" and Ehle "delectable" and the Tony voters went on to decide as much, too. On June 4, both stars and the revival itself collected trophies, marking the only time that a contemporary play has won actor and actress prizes for two sets of performers across two productions. Ehle's win was the more peculiar, simply because the competition in her category included her own mother, who was nominated for that season's premiere of a little-known Noël Coward play, *Waiting In the Wings*. "It was lovely - a dream come true," Rosemary Harris says of her daughter's victory. Ehle, for her part, remembers thinking, "Leave us alone; let us go home. I just want to go out for a curry with my mum." In any case, notes Ehle with appealing modesty, "Even though Glenn had won it and had been so wonderful, I never thought Annie was a Tony-winning part because she in so many ways is the supporting role; it's Henry's play."

But whereas other Donmar players - one thinks of Alan Cumming and Nicole Kidman - used their newfound Broadway perch to

Stephen Dillane in *The Real Thing* ▶

broaden their careers, Dillane at the end of the run packed up his Upper West Side rental apartment and brought his partner, Naomi Wirthner, and two sons straight home. What, then, did his New York theatre debut do for his profile? (In London, the actor's ever-spiralling regard within the industry landed him a starring role in Stoppard's 2002 National Theatre trilogy, *The Coast of Utopia*.) "I don't know," says Dillane, who would take a lot more than a Tony Award to get fussed by fame. "I just don't know. I never waited to find out."

66 I had directed at the Donmar during its in-between phase and, of course, attended so many performances there when it was the RSC back when I first came to London. It's just one of those theatres that you are thrilled to go to.

The space can be tricky, because it's on three sides, and it can be hard for the actor and the production to find a focus. But what can be a handicap is also a great asset: you do have fantastic contact with the audience because of the proximity and because of those three sides. And although there was a certain artifice to *Design For Living*, I wouldn't choose the Donmar for artificial work: You're just plain naked in there. **99**

SEAN MATHIAS, director
Design For Living, 1994
Suddenly Last Summer
(Warehouse Productions), 1999

Staircases have almost become a Donmar design constant, as shown via the sets for *Design For Living* ▲ and *The Little Foxes* ▶

viagra

chapter 6

"If we'd gone on like that, we would have both gone mad"

scene 5, "the Married Woman and the Politician," *The Blue Room*

"It was a big risk for them, too," Nicole Kidman is saying, reflecting upon the decision of the Donmar to mount her British stage debut, *The Blue Room*. "It could have been, 'What is Sam Mendes doing bringing this Australian actress over here?' Send her home."

Not bloody likely. For an evening defined at every turn by cool, no other Donmar production has generated *The Blue Room*'s quantity of heat.

Few, one can safely say, would cite the theatre's 1998 reworking of *La Ronde* as the best production of the Mendes regime. Or the emotionally densest. Or - notwithstanding the fuss it led to over nudity, specifically that of leading lady Kidman - even the sexiest. (On that last account, *The Real Thing*, a staging as fully clothed as *The Blue Room* was unbuttoned, is many Donmar regulars' production of choice.)

But there can be no doubt that *The Blue Room* has been the Donmar show to contain the most 'Mosts'. No production at this address prompted more advance buzz, received more headline-making commentary and reviews (one in particular), caused more of a Broadway stir and did more to widen the theatre's profile: so much so that one can speak of the Donmar's fortunes pre- and post-*Blue Room*.

For good - and, in some respects, for ill - David Hare's adaptation of the Arthur Schnitzler play became one of those rare theatre events far larger than itself. Reputations were made and revised as the play entered the wider cultural landscape, feeding a debate about celebrity casting in Britain that rages to this day. The irony is that so deeply atypical a Donmar project should have done so much to enlarge awareness of the theatre. In cast size alone, *The Blue Room* remains a Donmar anomaly: no other Mendes production was able to billet exactly one person each in the male and female dressing rooms, making fairly unnecessary the clause in Kidman's contract stipulating "exclusive use of a dressing room and a bathroom with shower." As the sole woman in a company of two, what other option was there?

The show was big box office and bigger news, and Mendes employs two highly dramatic images to encapsulate his experience of it. One is of a runaway train on which, he says, "in the end, I felt absolutely

◀ Charles Spencer, critic, Daily Telegraph

a passenger. I did not feel in any way that the train was driven by me or anyone else to do with the production." The other is of the lethal yet (in commercial terms) deliciously potent alien in Ridley Scott's 1979 film of the same name: "Like the alien in Ridley's movie, the play kind of lived inside the Donmar for a while, exploded out of its chest, left the theatre bleeding on a table somewhere gasping for breath, and was gone."

"It kind of felt like *The Blue Room* fed off us," continues Mendes. "We gave birth to it, and it left us all trailing in its wake. Something happened that was not to do with theatre." And that few participants at those late-summer rehearsals in Brixton could ever have envisaged.

❝ **The Blue Room was something I really really needed to do: it meant being in London, pushing myself and getting absorbed in work that wasn't something my husband had done or could advise me on or help me with at all. I felt very alone during the process, but that kind of established my love of what I do.**

I wear glasses - I'm a glasses girl - so when I take my glasses off, everything is blurry, which is really beneficial given that the front row at that theatre can be pretty intimidating. At the Donmar, it wasn't about, 'Let's just show up and get a pay cheque,' because you're working for no money; you're there because you love what you do, and nobody is motivated by anything beyond wanting to do something special. It's one of those places where you make friends.

I'm so glad if The Blue Room changed the Donmar's life, but I'm not sure I can take any of that credit. It's Sam and Caro who basically built play after play that changed it. I'm so glad The Blue Room was such a success for them. ❞

NICOLE KIDMAN, actress
The Blue Room, 1998

The project arose out of Mendes' desire to work with Kidman, marking an unusual instance of a Donmar venture deliberately structured around its lead. (The same was true of the 2001 revival of *The Little Foxes*, which wouldn't have happened without Penelope Wilton to play Regina.) Mendes had particularly admired the Australian actress's work in *To Die For*, the blackly comic 1995 Gus Van Sant movie that stands out early on amid a CV that *The Blue Room* - as Kidman is the first to admit - went on to transform. "That was the performance that made me want to work with Nicole as an actress," says Mendes. "It acknowledged and played upon the very thing that makes her unusual, which is this slightly unreachable, distant, cool sexuality; I thought she was spectacularly well-judged."

But it wasn't until the playwright Patrick Marber introduced Kidman and Mendes that talk began in earnest. Kidman wanted to do a play in London; the question was, which one? *Cat On A Hot Tin Roof* was an option, and would later be talked up as a Donmar or even a straight-to-Broadway vehicle to pair Kidman and her then-husband and frequent acting partner Tom Cruise: the idea was put paid to by (among other factors) the couple's divorce. "That would have been the obvious thing," Mendes says of *Cat*, citing a preference instead for Kidman in "something funky - a new play, relatively contemporary." If Kidman had got to know Marber via discussions about possibly appearing on Broadway in his hit play *Closer*, surely she could appear in London in something that packed a comparable up-to-the-minute charge.

It was while in England filming *Eyes Wide Shut* that Kidman was at the National Theatre to see

Nicole Kidman in *The Blue Room* ▶

Mendes' Cottesloe production of *Othello*. The director, seated a row behind, tapped her on the shoulder. And there began Mendes' appreciation of quite a separate person from the performer whom he had so admired on celluloid. "I was struck by the complete absolute difference between her screen persona and her real persona," says Mendes. "Nicole was very alive, very quick to laugh, without communicating that slight distance that she conveyed at the time on film."

Mendes wasted no time sending Kidman a John Barton version of *La Ronde* that had been produced in 1982 by the RSC . The aim was to familiarise the actress with a text that, Mendes felt, should be considered anew. At first, he thought of asking Marber to update it: "I felt duty-bound, since Patrick had introduced me to Nicole." But Marber declined, making the point, in Mendes' words, that the task "was too much like *Closer* in terms of being couplings in a contemporary city. Patrick felt he had written that play, and also that *Closer* hadn't yet had its full commercial life, so he would be competing with himself in the same territory."

The director next approached David Hare, with whom Mendes had never previously worked. "David in certain quarters has had a very rough ride," says Mendes, defending his choice of adaptor. "How many people stick their neck on the line with that degree of regularity on genuinely difficult contemporary issues? It doesn't happen. The bravery of the man, his sense of purpose, is not spoken of regularly: he's able to marry the political and the personal like no one else, really no one else."

At the same time, *The Blue Room* marked a significant departure for a playwright whose previous adaptations - whether Brecht (*The Life of Galileo, Mother Courage and Her Children*), Pirandello (*The Rules of the Game*), or Chekhov (*Ivanov*) - had stuck more closely to their source originals than Hare this time round would to Schnitzler. "This was unusual territory for David," says Mendes. "He so contextualises everything, and I was pulling him away from that; his trust was very moving to me."

Hare recalls the authorial challenge: "I felt a kind of primitive loyalty to playwrights that you shouldn't mess their work around - that

> " What was interesting to me doing two plays at the same theatre is that one was hugely successful and the other one wasn't and yet the support backstage and the atmosphere around the theatre were strikingly similar. I found that admirable, really. There was no sense doing *Here* that it was a flop and wasn't working out; we were committed to it and believed in it and enjoyed performing it. And the Donmar seemed proud to have it.
>
> The Donmar just has a magic to it; I'm not quite sure why. As an empty theatre, it seems ordinary, though it is so not ordinary when you perform on the stage. In a rehearsal room, you can pretty much go where you like, and it feels like that at the Donmar just because the audience is so close and on three sides. It feels very filmic when you're on that stage, though you have to be careful: whatever you're doing does have to be ping-ed out a little bit.
>
> There's a whole mood about the theatre that obviously has to do with doing wonderful plays with good directors. But it's also about people helping you out and making sure you have a good time. That's what creates the experience: You're getting paid diddlysquit but you don't begrudge it because the work is good and people look after you. "

IAIN GLEN, actor
Here, 1993
The Blue Room, 1998

STEPPING INTO FREEDOM

Schnitzler wrote in a certain period, and I had no right to rewrite it." What persuaded him otherwise was a return to the primary text. "When I read the scenes, I thought, these are better than I remember them." The task then became one of fulfilling Mendes' idea of a present-day version for two actors of the sexual daisy chain by Schnitzler that had spawned such diverse progeny as the celebrated Max Ophuls film of 1950 (itself remade twice over) and a much-lauded 1994 Off-Broadway musical, Michael John LaChiusa's *Hello Again*. In autumn, 2002, the Tricycle Theatre in northwest London premiered Irish dramatist Carlo Gebler's *10 Rounds*, a play said to have been inspired equally by the Ombudsman's Report into the Omagh Bombing in 1998 and by, you guessed it, *La Ronde*.

Schnitzler's drama is steeped in the world he knew, which is to say 1890s Vienna and a structure that ultimately comes back on itself, so that the play's first and last characters meet at the end: one person couples with another who couples with yet another and so on until you end up back at the person with whom you began. *The Blue Room*, then, retained Schnitzler's narrative circularity while locating the action in what Mendes defines as "a Kieslowskian European city - not specifically London but anywhere, so that there was a sense in which the world was very small and the blue room was the world": the idea was borne out by a poster image that showed a floating globe. Though placeless by choice, Hare's script anchored proceedings in certain cultural references of the day, among them *The Phantom of the Opera* and Madonna - the second of which got excised from the script at the Broadway performance of *The Blue Room* early in 1999 when Madonna was in fact in the audience (see show report, above).

Very early on, Hare would listen to his play read aloud across Mendes' kitchen table, Mendes taking the male roles and Lucy Davies, his assistant, the female ones. At the time, says Davies, who now works in development for the impresario Robert Fox (a Broadway co-producer of *The Blue Room*), "we all thought

---

Stage Manager's Report for: THE BLUE ROOM

Performance # 24

Date: January 6th, 1999

M T (W) TH F S SU Mat (Eve.)

ABSENT:

Curtain Up: 8:

Curtain Down: 9:

Running Time: 1:3

LATE:

INJURIES/ILLNESS:

REHEARSAL CALLS/WORK CALLS:

TECHNICAL:
After the matinee, Ed Diaz used the blue touch-up paint on some of the larger areas of the DSL walls that had gotten dirty.

PERFORMANCE:
A very good audience tonight and a strong show. As Madonna was in the audience tonight, Nicole cut the line in Scene 4 regarding Madonna's body-stocking for fear of the audience's response wrecking the scene. Nicole seemed to be feeling much better tonight.

Calling Stage Manager: David Hyslop

the play was what it was - a beautiful, elegant, conceit, and nothing more. It was obscene what happened to a chamber piece that in itself was so small."

The difficulty lay in unifying the material. Mendes and Hare decided against carrying over the narrator-figure of the ringmaster invented by Ophuls for his film and played by Anton Walbrook. "Why put in another character?" reasoned Mendes. In Hare's view, "the link, so to speak, had to be the five different parts each actor would play." To be sure, the young tart in the opening scene exists worlds away from the grandly self-dramatising actress who appears in the eighth and ninth of the play's ten liaisons: in between are an au pair, a married woman, and a model called Kelly, each with her own accent and referred to by what she is - the Actress etc. The connective tissue lay in the presence in her first stage appearance outside Australia of Kidman, opposite Scottish actor Iain Glen - a seasoned RSC alumnus who had appeared in the Donmar's very first season in Michael Frayn's ill-fated *Here*.

Kidman was aboard the project all along, having traded in one slab of Schnitzler for another: she came to the play fresh from the long and arduous experience filming *Eyes Wide Shut*, Stanley Kubrick's ice-cold and de-eroticising adaptation of Schnitzler's 1926 novella, *Dream Story*. (Kubrick, indeed, made one of his last public appearances at a performance of *The Blue Room* before his unexpected death in March, 1999.)

▲ Film director Stanley Kubrick leaves a London performance of *The Blue Room*, which starred Nicole Kidman, the leading lady of his final movie, *Eyes Wide Shut*

If Kidman's name was a constant, Glen wasn't Mendes' first thought any more than Hare had been: Rufus Sewell and, especially, Jude Law had come into the frame only to opt out for films. (Law would later in his career work alongside both Mendes and Kidman - directed by the former in *Road To Perdition* and starring opposite the latter in Anthony Minghella's *Cold Mountain*, the film version of the Charles Frazier best-seller.) But Mendes had admired Glen's *Henry V* for Matthew Warchus at the RSC and so returned to the actor who had earlier passed up the Donmar lead in *Company*.

Mendes rang Glen from America at his then-home in Greenwich to offer up the job. And though Glen was on the cusp of signing to do Trevor Nunn's National Theatre revival of *Betrayal*, he plumped for *The Blue Room* instead. "The very first time I read it, I was desperate to do it," recalls Glen, adding that Hare's script "buys into a lot of the things I enjoy as an actor of just having the opportunity to do different things within the framework of one piece." As a Shakespearean lead, Glen laughs, "I used to think, 'Oh, I wish I was doing Osric tonight.' You always feel the constraint of whatever role you're playing." Glen liked a range of roles encompassing a cocksure cabbie at the outset through to what Mendes had described as "a dashing Blairite New Labour politician" later on. (Rather more Gordon Brown, actually, in Glen's view, though the portrayal, he says, "got less Gordon Brownish" over time.)

The play "at its most basic," says Glen, "harks back to the true repertory days when an audience used to love to see actors do different roles within one season; I think that's quite sexy to an audience - they like that." And while film, he was well aware, "always tries to narrow you down and pigeonhole you into a type of role, *The Blue Room* celebrated versatility. The moment I read it, I rang Sam" - throwing an affectionate "you bastard," as Mendes recalls the phone call, into the conversation.

Kidman had her own reasons for tackling a play that did more than anything to assert her own independence and abilities as an actress apart from her status as a famous showbiz wife. For starters, she had got to know the London theatre landscape well during her time (five years on and off) spent in the capital shooting *The Portrait of A Lady* and then *Eyes Wide Shut* and being with Cruise while he made *Mission: Impossible*. "When Tom was working, I would go to the theatre; that's what I would do," says Kidman, who had last appeared on stage as Shelby - Julia Roberts' film role - in a 1988 Sydney production of *Steel Magnolias*. As a member of the Donmar audience, Kidman had seen *Cabaret* and, five years on, the Pinter triple-bill. Later still, it was while walking Patrick Marber's dog that Kidman realised to what extent she and the British theatre were potential kin: "I just loved the sensibility of the English playwrights and also the directors and the spirit of the English theatre."

As a child growing up in Australia, she had been steeped in live performance, including modern dance (a favourite of her father): "My parents were just obsessed with it. I was taken to the theatre since I was five - to stuff I didn't understand and that I couldn't grasp and yet where I could still enjoy the spectacle." She wanted to pass on the same appreciation to her children, Connor and Isabella, who were three and five at the time of *The Blue Room*: "Anything that puts them in contact with human reality and takes them away from the TV." (Recalling a complaint from Connor that he was bored, his mother was quick to reply, "That's your fault.")

Mendes describes early in their acquaintanceship feeling Kidman's need to "strike out on some level," not least after the hermetic intensity of an *Eyes Wide Shut* shoot that took Kidman and Cruise the better part of two years. The couple, notes Mendes, "had lost any sense of where they lived and what they did for a living, and both wanted to strike out afterwards in acts of self-expression; they went off and did, really, their own thing" - the movie *Magnolia* in Cruise's case; the theatre in Kidman's.

As a result, the actress said 'yes' the minute discussions with Mendes led to *The Blue Room*, adapted by a writer whom Kidman already knew. She and Hare had met socially through, among others, Warren Hoge, the New York Times' London bureau chief. On another occasion, film director Fred Schepisi, who directed Hare's screenplay of *Plenty*, had organised a lunch. Why her enthusiasm for the venture? "I was in a position where I just wanted to," says Kidman, emphasizing that her decision came before "everyone was doing theatre." (Juliette Binoche and Kevin Spacey had, but not yet Daryl Hannah, Macaulay Culkin, or Matt Damon, among the many other starry visitors who would follow Kidman to the London stage.) "I said to Sam, 'Oh, that sounds terrifying, but OK; I'm in.' That's usually how I make a decision: it's very instinctual. It was based on knowing David already and just thinking Sam was wonderful."

66 **Whenever one does a show at the Donmar, it is always fantastically enjoyable. You feel like the whole building is humming towards the production - it's not like having a floor of sponsorship and a floor of development and they don't know what's going on. They all know you; it's like working with a family, really.**
Sam has immense savoir faire and cool, and he's a fantastic producer: he can dispel any animosity with just this great cloud of bonhomie. And my God can he busk it when I know he has come to a meeting unprepared; he knows how to wing it.
Sam has always been the same person across all three shows we've done together, but now is the time of the international accolades. I'm looking forward to *Twelfth Night* and *Uncle Vanya*: I haven't worked with him since he has been hailed as the best thing since moving picture sound. 99

MARK THOMPSON, designer
Company, 1995
The Front Page, 1997
The Blue Room, 1998
Uncle Vanya (costumes), 2002
Twelfth Night (costumes), 2002

Before anything else could happen, she and Glen obviously had to meet and start forming the bond that would see the pair through a jointly demanding seven months. As homework, Mendes told Kidman to watch the 1990 movie *Mountains of the Moon*, the period drama from Bob Rafelson signalling an early bid on Glen's part for a film renown that had for whatever reason not quite taken hold. Then came the official introduction at Mendes' Primrose Hill flat, an evening all three participants vividly recollect.

Mendes: "I talked nonstop the first twenty minutes because I was so nervous and wanted them to get on. I remember perching on the arm of my sofa and rabbiting on."

Glen: "I remember the very first time climbing the steps into Sam's flat, and Nicole was already there. Sam immediately went, 'All right; I'm just off for a wee,' and went to the loo, and I sat in a chair at the opposite end of the room. Then I sat beside Nicole on the sofa and just remember saying, 'Well, goodness,' and we laughed very very quickly. We both just said, 'Oh fuck, this could be really dreadful, but if we come unstuck, we come unstuck together.'"

Kidman: "I'm dreadfully shy and came in and was so shy I could hardly speak. I kept feeling like I was going to vomit: I had heard how brilliant Iain was on stage, and he was formidable just as a person. I thought, I'm out of my league, but he really was so gentle and kind to me. He took my hand - not literally - and guided me through it, saying 'Don't worry; I'm not going to let you fall.'"

A meal followed at Limani in Regent's Park Road, the Greek restaurant that was to become the trio's unofficial haunt - so much so that its proprietor became fond of remarking to all and sundry that "Sam fucking Mendeles (sic) was in here with that Nicole Kidman." The memory makes Mendes smile.

And though he clearly could have taken the project anywhere given Kidman's box office cred, the director was determined that *The Blue Room* remain a Donmar venture. "It was a play about physical intimacy, and I needed an intimate space in which to do it. Also, I was aware Nicole needed to take baby steps initially, having left the stage all those years ago. Every couple of weeks, Nicole would ring and go, 'Oh my God, are we really going to do this?' But so much of a director's job is to give people a belief in themselves."

"My instincts always told me Nicole could do it," says Mendes, "that she could pull it off."

Rehearsals took place in south London in premises formerly used by London Weekend Television. Instead of the usual five weeks, Mendes had scheduled an extra sixth: "to give Nicole time," he says, not least for voice work with Patsy Rodenburg in order to strengthen muscles that had gone un-exercised for years.

Rodenburg, very much a star practitioner in her field, remembers meeting a star in Kidman who was ready to work. "When you work with somebody who hasn't done a huge amount of theatre, the first worry is, 'Will they work? Are they diligent enough?' Nicole did everything one asked so that was a tremendous relief. She has a lot of fun, a lot of joy in her."

Vocal matters aside, the rehearsals were equally geared toward physical demands, with Mendes introducing massage into the rehearsal room because, reports Glen, "he wanted us to be physically more comfortable." Hence the group massage, Mendes and stage manager Kate Chate included, which, Glen adds deadpan, "we rather enjoyed." (Also enjoyable: the Tupperware sushi lunches from Nobu, proffered by Kidman, that became a midday staple.)

At the same time, it wasn't easy making sense of a series of individual playlets as opposed to one organic, through written whole: Hare had done eleven drafts before feeling that he had struck the proper tone. Mendes, in turn, found himself remarking to assistant director Sacha Wares on the fact that "the play doesn't work; it doesn't engage, and if it engages, it deliberately disengages ten minutes later." Nor was Hare necessarily available to act as problem-solver since he was busy with his own rehearsals for *Via Dolorosa*, a solo show culled from his travels to the Middle East. Hare was making a supremely daunting acting debut in this play, which - as timing would have it - had scheduled its opening at the Duke of York's a fortnight before *The Blue Room* premiere up the road. Mendes, Glen, and Kidman made a group outing early on to *Via Dolorosa*. Their reaction? "When we saw David, it was David on stage," says Glen, chuckling as he recounted one particular remark from Hare to his *Blue Room* cast. "David told us, 'You're only doing five characters each; I'm doing one hundred.'" (In truth, thirty-three.)

Hare speaks of being otherwise occupied as *The Blue Room* was put on its feet: "It was ghastly. There was a very intense rehearsal period with Sam and Nicole and Iain, and they were very, very close, and because I was only going in at odd intervals, it was hard for me to be part of the way the work developed." When Hare was there, he would sit with his computer, scripting changes on the spot. The odd flare-up was known to occur.

Not that levity was by any means absent. Lighting designer Hugh Vanstone, whose work on *The Blue Room* and *The Unexpected Man* went on to win him that season's Olivier Award, recalls the mirth generated by Mendes' encyclopaedic command of children's TV programs (Dick Dastardly, Penelope Pitstop etc.), complete with requisite sound effects. And then in would walk Hare on a particular day and, says Vanstone, "it was like, teacher's here: behave!" Mendes and Penelope Pitstop? "I was a child brought up entirely on TV," explains the director, unembarrassed, "and I've got a garbage bin for a brain."

Glen was among those who didn't mind having Hare "a little away" as the play was coming together. "I knew David well" - the actor had met a brutal end opposite Charlotte Rampling in writer-director Hare's 1988 film, *Paris By Night* - "and was aware that writers can be protective of their lines when what Sam wanted was to shake things up. We could be honest when David wasn't there. As an actor, you have to try and possess a play yourself and realise it in your own way."

Kidman was busy allaying her own demons. "I had absolute terror during the lead-up to rehearsals. I was there the week before, starting to grapple with the accents and thinking, 'What am I doing? This is crazy.' Sam manages to keep you feeling very safe, and yet there I was feeling, 'This is madness,' and I got really frightened."

Glen recalls a rehearsal period "where we just flew with it very quickly" before hitting a brick wall that it took time and additional trust to break through. "I'm not sure how much of this we shared with Sam, but we ground to a terrible halt round about the middle of rehearsals where Nicole and I lost faith. I think we thought there was a terrible danger that the play would just be Nicole and Iain kind of getting off with each other throughout an evening, and it would be very, very irritating for people. We weren't comfortable with it."

The actors needed to shake off any self-consciousness so they could inhabit five different people and ten different pairings. "You can't wander around being vaguely Nic" - his nickname for Kidman - "and vaguely Iain throughout an evening, and that's what we felt we were doing. The main thing we had to do was really, really differentiate the parts, so that they all had different energies and different voices and different physicalities." Hare offered an assist by agreeing to Kidman's request that the Model in scenes six and seven be made Australian, so that the actress could speak at least one role in her natural accent.

But the part Kidman found trickiest, perhaps surprisingly, was the Actress, the richly self-assured diva who appears toward the end of the play *in flagrante* first with a playwright, then with an aristocrat. But Kidman *is* an actress, so how hard could the assignment be? "Yeah," she laughs, "but not that kind of actress. To go big like that was not something I had ever done; Sam really had to exercise me on that." References of sorts helped, including a celebrated Snowdon photograph of Helen Mirren that, says Hare, "caught completely the incredible wilful sensuality of a performer. We used to look at that picture because it fully represented an actress in the best sense - it was just completely timeless." A portrait of Mirren leaning into a mirror, her cleavage showing, the shot, says Mendes, "was very sexy and powerful."

As the Actress clicked into place, says Mendes, Kidman's entire performance did, too. "Nicole had to learn that you can be loud and theatrical - theatrical in gesture as well as truthful. Once she mastered the Actress, the others all gradually came to life." Hare seconds the opinion. "I think Nicole was so sort of nervous, being a film actress where 'truth' is everything and extravagance is very rare. And actually, the Actress was the part in which she was completely wonderful."

Glen himself acknowledged that "there were times well into rehearsals when Nicole wasn't comfortable and wasn't realising some of the more demonstrative characters like the Actress. I was doing huge overacting to try and compensate because Nicole was coming under the radar; she didn't know what she was doing, and refused to pretend that she did." How, then, did the pair cope? Patience and

perseverance: "Nicole is such a quick learner that she doesn't need anything told twice. She was totally dogged during rehearsal and works harder than anyone I've ever worked with. That was true throughout the run."

Whatever concerns she had about her own contribution, the communality of the rehearsal process greatly appealed to Kidman. She and Cruise had been living on a private road (crucial for security purposes) near Regent's Park only for Kidman to find herself working south of the river, her presence very much part of a team. "Some of my greatest memories were being in Brixton in the middle of a heatwave and making tea in a little tearoom with the RSC next door. It was just about the work; there was no luxury - no one carrying on about this or that. The whole thing just sort of disciplines you: everyone was trying to make it work."

And yet, if Kidman had her head down, the rest of the world was beginning to perk up. Press interest was first ignited by Baz Bamigboye in his weekly Friday column in the Daily Mail, which broke the news of Kidman's casting on June 19, ten days before the theatre had planned its own announcement. "This will distract enormously from the opening of our new play, *How I Learned To Drive*," fumed Donmar general manager Nick Frankfort in an internal memo.

❝ The Donmar is so intimate that you actually can get away with lighting someone's face with a candle on that stage, and that is what is so special: you really feel as if you are in the room with the people who are acting for you. Yes, there are challenges because it is so small, but on the whole it's a liberating space. Strangely, even ironically, your vocabulary is increased because you can get away with so little.

I've often gone in with ideas that are slightly too grand for the space - too stagey or theatrical. One is constantly reminded of the power of simplicity. **❞**

HUGH VANSTONE, lighting designer

Insignificance, 1995
The Front Page, 1997
The Blue Room, 1998
Juno and the Paycock, 1999
Orpheus Descending, 2000
Uncle Vanya, 2002
Twelfth Night, 2002

At the same time, faxes were arriving from Los Angeles on an order that the Donmar - which had never previously employed an international film star - wasn't used to. In August, Kidman's publicist in LA, Lee Anne Haigney, wrote Frankfort providing her Federal Express account number so that any items and autograph requests left for Kidman at the theatre could be sent on to America. The exception, stage manager Kate Chate allowed in a separate note to Donmar staff, were "very important people" (Richard Eyre and the Queen were cited by name) where it was OK "to approach Nicole directly."

Throughout the run, Kidman was to have on hand her friend and personal assistant of five years, Felicia Bushman, whom the Overseas Labour Service approved in the same batch of work permits as one Nicole Mary Kidman. Bushman was to enter the country under the employ not of the Donmar but of Kidman, who handwrote a letter to that effect. (Rather touchingly, the letter mis-spells Donmar Warehouse as Wharehouse - the subliminal influence, perhaps, of Kidman playing a prostitute in *The Blue Room*'s first and also final scenes.) Meanwhile, Kidman's agents at CAA had sent across a four-page missive setting forth the mutually agreed terms by which their client would appear on the Donmar stage. "We understand that the dressing rooms at the Donmar are relatively understated and plain but functional," the document made clear, as if conceding an unspoken point: clearly the message of what the Donmar was - and wasn't (i.e. a venue open to demands for redecoration) - had got through early on.

And while Kidman's PR firm PMK was advising London photographer Mark Douet of its standard photographic agreement - in essence, that the artist gets to choose the shots - publicist Joy Sapieka was scheduling a scant three interviews (a drop in the request bucket) for Kidman. It was agreed that she would talk to Bamigboye, the Evening Standard's Hot Tickets, and Jane Edwardes of Time Out, the venue of choice being the Union Club in Soho, where Kidman was a member. Advance coverage, says Mendes, was "deliberately contained." A grateful Kidman confirms: "The Donmar really protected me."

Eventually, however, it was time for *The Blue Room* to leave behind the relative seclusion of Brixton and what Kidman looks back on as "so tiny a group of people: just Iain, Sam, and I." And that meant finally delivering the glimpse of flesh from Kidman in scene seven that would go on to become - in news terms - a global sensation.

The moment is easily overlooked on the page, where Hare's stage directions read simply: the Model gets dressed. Occurring nearly three-fourths of the way through the evening, the action requires the Model to follow a passionate kiss from the Playwright by standing up, back to the audience, and putting on her underwear while the Playwright assists by helping with her top. A rueful exchange ensues about happiness, though one wonders over time how many in the audience heard it having just witnessed what a salivating press clearly found unthinkable: Nicole Kidman in the flesh had appeared, well, in the flesh.

There was, of course, an alternative: the Model could have dressed under a sheet, an option Mendes dismissed as "ridiculously coy." Instead, the director told Kidman, "probably the best thing to do is just stand up and pull on your knickers. I said, 'I guarantee you it will be very, very intimate and lit by the candles.' Nicole said fine, she would do it in the tech [the technical run through at the theatre that precedes the dress rehearsal] but she didn't want to do it in the naked light of the rehearsal room; that would be a bit exposing. So she got to the tech and did it."

Kidman remembers the courage required to do so . "I was shy and kept going, 'Oh, I don't have the right underwear'; I always came up with some sort of excuse. Finally, Sam just said, 'Nicole, here we go. I think it's very important; I don't think it's exploitative. It's totally character-driven.'" (It no doubt helped that the black knickers were lent to the production by Kidman herself, along with some flesh-coloured g-strings that - the production costume list made sure to point out - the performer "sometimes wears home. If your stock gets low, ask Felicia to replenish your supply.") The act itself, reflects Kidman, "was a very sweet moment, and it was that simple. He dresses her, and it's sort of gentle when he puts her top on; she's like a little doll to him."

Lighting man Hugh Vanstone was impressed with Kidman's apparent ease once she came to do the scene. "Nicole was truly professional and as grown-up about that as she was about everything else; there was no hoo-ha." Prompting rather more cause for concern were the numerous technical requirements - scene changes, music cues, and the like - for what remains one of the most logistically complex Donmar shows to date. (*Company* and *Habeas Corpus*, by contrast, had far larger casts but a single set.) At 11pm the night before the first preview, Mendes got everyone's approval to work on into the early hours of the morning, with stage hands busily shifting furniture manually that would later be conveyed in and out on tracks for the Broadway production: audiences there are less kindly disposed to watching stagehands dressed in black busily setting each scene. The alternative to the last-minute late-night activity would be to cancel a performance. And that was a move which Mendes, no doubt accurately, felt would give out the wrong signals - namely, that Kidman wasn't ready, when in fact it was the technical demands that were the genuinely pressing problem.

The Blue Room began performances on schedule September 10 in advance of a September 22 opening

- a longish preview period by Donmar standards. (Mendes' earlier *Front Page*, by contrast, had its press night within mere days of starting previews.) And while London was getting ready to feast on what came to be known as Kidmania, rife with the accompanying Tom Cruise sightings and the like, Glen was among those confronting the discrepancy between a relentless media glare and what was, he felt, "the mundane truth: *The Blue Room* was just another play."

Glen, too, was demonstrating commendable cool amid the ever-building amount of paparazzi who had come to profit off his colleague. His sangfroid lay in an ability from the outset to take Kidman for who she was, unencumbered by a sense of starriness that the actress, in any case, doesn't project. "Those concerns, if I had any, got broken down very very quickly, and, of course, Nicole is not somebody who would promote any kind of distance and aloofness." A sign of enormous self-possession on Glen's part? Without a doubt, says Mendes, who describes the production as "a test of character for Iain that he came through with flying colours; he could easily have been emasculated, basically, by the experience, but he was completely phlegmatic about it. Also he really, truly liked and admired Nicole and felt thrilled for her - that she was becoming her own person through this whole process."

"Iain was incredibly gorgeous and calm and careful with Nicole," recalls Mark Thompson, the set and costume designer responsible for what he terms the "Yves Klein blue" (the reference is to the colour palette of the French avant-garde painter) that defined the show visually. Kidman responded, in Thompson's view, "by putting an enormous amount of trust in Iain."

Glen deflects any praise in his handling of the situation towards Kidman and towards the democratising process of making theatre at the Donmar. "I don't know if it's a matter of confidence or not, but I utterly treated *The Blue Room* like any other play and that Nic was a film star became irrelevant very, very quickly. She wasn't a film star: she was somebody who was trying to be a prostitute and my wife and a model and her name was Nicole." In any case, reports Glen, "very soon after you get inside a rehearsal room with another actor, and the other actor's good, you engage so with the storytelling and the lines and everything you're dealing with in rehearsals that the stuff around it loses its power."

The point is, Glen remembers as *Blue Room* public performances approached, "we weren't thinking about anything beyond trying to do the best we could. I mean, for a lot of the rehearsal, we had been

▲ David Hare

thinking we don't want to do this." The truth: "we had no expectation of it." Kidman records a comparable panic. "I remember saying to Sam before we opened, 'I'm not going to be good; I'm not good, and I'm so terrified of letting you down.'" Hare then had his own concerns based on a dress rehearsal at which, he says, Kidman's inexperience was all too plain to see. So doubtful was the playwright that he distrusted his own Nicole - Hare's wife, designer Nicole Farhi - who had come back from a preview to record that Kidman was "unbelievably adept."

Says Hare: "I said no no no; I don't think that can be right, since the Nicole I'd seen had been looking so nervous." It wasn't until a subsequent matinee - one of the few performances available to Hare, who was by then well into his *Via Dolorosa* run at the Duke of York's - that *The Blue Room*'s author was able to judge for himself: "I couldn't believe anybody had learned so much in a week. I had never seen a faster learning curve."

Lucy Davies won't soon forget Kidman's very first curtain call. "Nicole's eyes widened like an eight-year-old: she had done it, and it was great, and there they [the audience] all were." Kidman, for her part, was of two minds even about how to bow. "I had to be told how to do the curtain call, so I wasn't sort of apologising for the performance in my bow. It's a strange thing: you have to be able to go, 'Thank you.' And it can be quite confronting, because it's the first time you come out as yourself."

Come opening night, and Kidman had at last to confront the press. Afterwards, while verdicts were being penned, upwards of two hundred people had convened at One Aldwych in the hotel's lower-ground Axis restaurant for a party hosted by hotelier Gordon Campbell Gray, a Donmar devotee. (Campbell Gray, indeed, threw an all-night Academy Awards party in the basement screening room in March, 2001, in honour of Mendes' *American Beauty* Oscar bid - successful, of course - for best director.) The Donmar contributed £500 to the bash - "a mere drop in the ocean, frankly," as Caro Newling put it at the time - which more than paid for itself in terms of the press attention paid to Kidman and Cruise alone.

> **"** I'm not fond of the space. I find the Donmar very difficult to design for and very hard to focus in. I find its flatness bleak. I don't think it's a great theatre space, compared with the Royal Court or the Almeida; it's not actually one of the more charming or play-suited playhouses. I often think the Donmar has prospered in spite of the space instead of because of it: one spends an awful lot of time looking at the rest of the audience across what seems a big empty featureless characterless stage.
>
> There is something special about the Donmar in the sense of being close to the actors, although *The Blue Room* would have been fantastic in any intimate theatre. When I saw the play at the Minerva in Chichester, that seemed a better place to present it; that was an enchanted space to do *The Blue Room* in. **"**
>
> **DAVID HARE**, playwright
> The Blue Room, 1998

And though Kidman and Cruise would later part company, Kidman's then-spouse was very much a part of *The Blue Room* experience. More often than not, he would watch performances from the glassed-in prompt corner stage right so that his presence wouldn't be a distraction. (There probably isn't another major London theatre where spectators are quite so aware of one another.) "Whenever he came," says Mendes, "Tom was visibly proud of Nicole and in awe of the courage it took not only to do this play in the first place but to do it in such a small space, so close to people and nakedly vulnerable." On one

Evening Standard, September 1998

**"I don't care if it's a six-hour adaptation of *Waiting for Godot*,
as long as it's got that Kidman in it."**

occasion, Cruise even lent a hand, supplying a pair of night vision binoculars for the deputy stage manager to help through a particularly dark (hence, tricky) scene change. Says lighting man Hugh Vanstone: "Tom's night vision specs saved the day." Demonstrating her own appetite for the space was the couple's young daughter, Isabella, who liked to stand on stage before the show, soaking up the ambience. "I'd think," remembers Kidman, "oh, now she's getting a taste."

So, too, was London for its neophyte stage star. On September 23, with only standing places left to sell, the theatre found itself housing not just a popular but a critical hit, justifying a £213,000 advance sale as of opening night that remains among the largest at the Donmar to date. Whatever reservations existed about the play (and there were plenty) were swept aside in collective adoration of its leading lady. "I knew Ms. Kidman was beautiful," wrote Robert Gore-Langton, setting the tone in his Daily Express review. "But in the flesh she is tall, blonde, mint-cool and just eye-sockingly, jaw-droppingly, head-swimmingly gorgeous." Those very remarks resurfaced unexpectedly at a subsequent prize-giving ceremony for Mendes in Salzburg where, amid an honourary citation read entirely in German, a language the director does not speak, Mendes did recognise words like "eye-sockingly" and "jaw-droppingly" that had been culled from the Express review. Meanwhile, what did the same critic make of Kidman's acting? "In fact," said Gore-Langton, "she's superb. I honestly can't think of a British actress who would have done it better." (The Spectator's Sheridan Morley could, offering up Jane Asher and Felicity Kendal as preferable alternatives.) But it was Charles Spencer in the Daily Telegraph - in a comment he later said had been added as an afterthought to lend "zing to a rather flat ending" - whose overnight notice contained that once-in-a-lifetime phrase that has gone on to enter the lexicon. Capping a near-confessional of a review in which Spencer admitted to having "eyes on stalks" for its visiting star, *The Blue Room*, he wrote, was "pure theatrical Viagra." And so its onward journey to Broadway was assured.

It scarcely mattered that the guiding affect of the play was in many people's unstalked eyes - mine included - precisely the opposite. As Georgina Brown wrote in the Mail On Sunday: "This is definitely not theatrical Viagra, which is perhaps the sad, sly point being made. It is sex as shopping - a heartless transaction." Such remarks were, however, very quickly beside the point confronted with what Mendes terms "the naked self-revelation involved in the London reviews that were almost naively innocent. There was a kind of, 'to-hell-with it; I'm just going to tell you what I think' quality," says Mendes. The glamour of the moment seemed to have swept aside serious analysis. But as indices of the middle-aged male critical mind set, this collection of reviews has not been equalled since.

Broadway had always been the hoped-for destination for the production, which was mounted at the Donmar with £50,000 enhancement money from New York's Shubert Organization - a sum that Caro Newling looks on as "our first first-look deal, as it were." And so it was that Broadway's most powerful theatre owners ended up housing the play at the Cort Theatre on West 48th Street for an engagement nearly twice the length of the London one. And in a theatre some four times the size. And at a capitalization of $1.5 million, a difference made doubly significant by the inclusion within the Donmar's £94,000 pre-production budget for the same play of "everything," says Newling, "down to the postage stamps."

In London, meanwhile, the nudity issue - far from abating - had only intensified interest in a play where tickets were going on the black market for ten or twenty times their face value. Scarcely had the show opened and been somewhat coolly reviewed by Evening Standard critic Nicholas de Jongh (the best aspect of the evening, he felt, was Kidman, whose "five roles are in her elegant, confident grasp") before the same paper featured a thorough going over of Kidman's body by columnist Shane Watson. That was an all-stops-out rave: "We knew she wasn't fat, we knew she'd look pretty good, but this! A figure (narrow hips, bosoms at armpit level, long rangy legs, no - repeat, no - cellulite or any interruptions to the all-over moonstone skin) that not only matches up to the best but would be exceptional on a 20-year-old. Whereas Nicole is 31."

Whew!

Wherever possible, the same paper would run a photo of Kidman from the play in fishnet tights, whether appropriate to the accompanying article or not. "You Know When You've Been Kidman-ed," trumpeted the headline to a second Shane Watson column less than a week after the earlier one: this time about the star's apparent habit of buying in bulk. Three days later, the Standard's entire page three saw the wigged Kidman yet again, on that occasion accompanying an eye-catching piece about tough-to-obtain tickets: "If you've always dreamed of seeing Nicole Kidman, dream on."

David Hare took a bemused view of the single mindedness of the press, which included an art review from Natasha Walter in the Observer that found Kidman's name amid a consideration of that season's John Singer Sargent exhibition at the Tate (now, the Tate Britain): Kidman's presence at a preview of the show, wrote Walter, was making it hard to focus on the actual art. "Like Princess Diana or David Beckham, all this became simply a way to sell newspapers," says Hare, who had skilfully anatomised Fleet Street over a decade before in *Pravda*, his play co-written with Howard Brenton. The playwright had developed a theory that, post-Princess Diana, Kidman and Cruise were the show-biz aristocracy required by a needy and capricious press that has since moved on to Britney Spears, Anna Kournikova, and the like.

Or has it? Nearly four years later, the Standard's near-obsession with Kidman showed no sign of easing up. "Let's all do the Kidman cover-up," blared a July 2, 2002, headline. The relevant article by health and fitness writer Gita Mendis advised readers, "You won't catch Nicole exposing her fair skin to the sun. Nor should the rest of us." As for her exposure on the Donmar stage, the public couldn't get enough - even if it was the lesser-known Glen who was, in truth, baring far more, starting with a stark-naked cartwheel in full light that made a dimly backlit Kidman seem doubly demure. "Iain was a showstopper on stage," says Lucy Davies, "with and without his clothes on."

The disparity in attention wasn't lost on either performer. "It certainly did seem strange to me to focus on the female nudity and not as much on the male nudity," says Kidman, especially, she says, with "Iain looking quite spectacular, I might add; I'd say, 'Iain, you look amazing.'"

"It did make us laugh," says Glen, hypothesizing that the shadowy nature of Kidman's nakedness may have added to its appeal. "Nicole was much cleverer, being elusive and hidden, so of course that was much more interesting - apart from the fact that she's a very, very beautiful woman as opposed to me wandering around. The male organ is not a particularly attractive appendage at the best of times." The sexual act itself was indicated by a series of blackouts accompanied by back wall projections - the latter, a Mendes idea not in the script - chronicling the particular time involved: from twenty-eight seconds to one hour forty-five minutes. No miming of the activity, then, in the best (or perhaps not) tradition of Terry Johnson's stage version of *The Graduate,* with its visible scramblings beneath the sheets? "No thank you," says Mendes. "And Iain and Nicole aren't actually *doing* it, so how can you possibly persuade people otherwise?" He thought of his solution as a cinematic jump cut.

None of which kept the performers from being likened to a sexual stimulant, a potentially dehumanising comparison that they took in their stride. "I thought, 'I'll accept that,'" says Glen, who found himself basking in a post-Viagra afterglow. "I won't knock that comment back; that will do. It implied people believed in our chemistry, and that was good, since if they didn't, the play was not going to work."

"I was just so relieved," says Kidman, "because so much of being an actor is the fear of letting everybody else down." In critical terms, it seemed, Kidman was toughest on herself, as Richard Gere was among those to discover firsthand. One night, Glen recalls, Gere came backstage and said to Nicole, "'That was absolutely wonderful,' and she was saying, 'It wasn't; it was fucking awful,' and Richard joked and said, 'That's what I meant; it was fucking awful. It just came out wrong.'" Glen's point: "There were very few performances Nicole would finish and think, 'That felt good.' She was hard on herself."

Nonetheless, and notwithstanding a somewhat slavering press, the London run turned out to be a happy experience for its creators, with the play at no point better, Mendes felt, than once it had settled into its Donmar stride. The director cites "the telepathic, very intimate relationship" that Kidman and Glen developed during the two-month London gig. The communication between them, he says, "was so

Iain Glen as the Aristocrat in *The Blue Room* ▶

delicate and gentle," with the Donmar's famed capacity for allowing a spectator to eavesdrop showing itself as a real strength. Kidman staked her claim to an absorption into all things English by agreeing to appear as Sue Lawley's guest on Desert Island Discs. Both within the Donmar's walls and beyond them, it seemed, she had arrived.

The actors at every turn entered into the spirit of the venue, Kidman's chattiness winning over the crew even as her largesse toward Glen - on opening night, she gave him a mountain bike - testified to their burgeoning friendship. ("Sam got slightly in despair," Glen says, recalling his excitement about the present, "because I wouldn't stop fiddling with the bike. He would say, 'Isn't it time to get into costume?'") During the play's final week, the pair agreed on the Monday to meet a group of visiting New Yorkers for a brief post-show chat. The following evening was the show's Donmar fund-raising gala: a benefit performance with an early start followed by a champagne reception with the cast at The Ivy just minutes away; the event raised £37,500 for the theatre. That restaurant, meanwhile, had become a Kidman hangout: "I remember thinking, 'God, I can get a table at The Ivy; the show must be going well.'"

The satisfaction spread to the Donmar staff, who were delighted to discover someone with whom they could get on. At the time, Lucy Ryan was the person in charge of things like house seats, so it fell to her one day to tell the Duke of Westminster that there were no more *Blue Room* tickets to be had. (His reply, says Ryan: "'That's a bit rich, considering I own the land your theatre is on.'") But, says Ryan, "because Nicole was happy, everyone around her was happy. If she had been unhappy, the whole atmosphere would have been completely different. She was surrounded by a very well-oiled machine which slotted into our well-oiled machine. We had to do a lot of preparation to get her" - hiring a front-of-house security guard, for instance - "but we weren't any different because she was there." Theatre manager Julia Christie recalls Kidman carrying on with the run despite an eye infection: "She was about the most beautiful woman I had ever met; I thought, I'd die to look like you and have eyes like that."

In Hollywood, word had spread that a tiny studio theatre across the Atlantic could do good things for a resting film star. So it was not long before Mendes was fielding enquiries in the "double digits" from various big names who, says the director, "were looking to do a play in London to ignite or, as it were, alter their careers, or their perception of their careers, and thought we might be interested in housing them." (Some have ended up coming under other auspices.) Instead, the Donmar very specifically took the non-celebrity route of reviving *The Real Thing* for Stephen Dillane. "The notion that we would somehow take what we can get - grab any passing celebrity and push them through the theatre doors to read the telephone directory - is absolute nonsense. Nicole was a very specific choice that I had made about someone I wanted to work with."

October 31 saw the end of *The Blue Room*'s Donmar run but not of Kidman's generosity. By way of thanks, Caro Newling, Joy Sapieka, and Patsy Rodenburg all received pashminas - Newling's, she says, "bigger than my whole house." Others got champagne, a coffee machine, a pair of roller blades: "every gift," per Newling, "so absolutely precise." In addition to a vase later on, designer Mark Thompson was also given a pair of trainers halfway through the run. "Nicole said to me, 'you've got to have this pair that Tom just bought.'" And within weeks, the production had shifted to New York and to the largest advance sale for a straight play in Broadway history: $3.8 million, exceeding by some $400,000 the hefty amount that Judi Dench in Hare's own *Amy's View* would open to in New York four months later. (The record has since been superseded only by *The Graduate* on Broadway, which opened in April, 2002, to a cash advance of $5 million, according to its co-producer Sacha Brooks.)

Gone, too, were the £250 a week pay cheques (about $400) that had made their own headlines for Kidman as regards what in London was inevitably a money-losing venture for the actress ; in New York, she and Glen were paid $2,000 a week each, with Kidman on a customary (for Broadway) back-end deal that boosted her pay packet accordingly once the production recouped - which took about six weeks.

As a Broadway newcomer, Kidman was probably the most excited about transferring the play to New York, even if she would share the general concern at the lack of intimacy to the American staging that became a collective complaint: "You're 14, and you kind of go, New York, Broadway: I'm so glad to actually have had that occur. Whatever else happens in my life, I can actually say, 'I did Broadway.'" What's more, Kidman points out, "because we were sold out, we didn't have to worry about, 'Is this going to play? Are we going to have a run?' That was the beauty of it."

Less beautiful was the inevitable down side accompanying any show that reaches Broadway rife with expectation, not least fed by a New York Magazine spread advising Broadway theatregoers where to sit at the Cort Theatre in order to catch the best view of Kidman's bare bum. In England, says Kidman, the event seemed "more about the play and about the whole experience of the play; in New York, it was, 'She stands there naked for ten seconds, seen from behind.' I mean, please." In Glen's view, "the furore around the play tended to be of a positive nature, even if it was misguided and smutty. At least it wasn't, 'Don't go to this because it's a complete waste of time.' It had a positive feel to it; it was such a high."

The fact is, the performers emerged from the New York run rather better than Mendes or Hare, the latter of whom would end up having three plays on Broadway in one season, starting with *Blue Room* and then *Via Dolorosa* and finally *Amy's View*. (Of the trio, *Via Dolorosa* was easily the best reviewed, though Judi Dench in *Amy's View* did win the Best Actress Tony.) But it's illustrative of the differing response to *The Blue Room* in the two capitals that whereas the play's Donmar incarnation got six Olivier nominations, its Broadway version wasn't nominated for a single Tony. So mindful was London of *The Blue Room* even in the play's absence that Kidman and Glen flew back to London for twenty-four hours during Broadway previews so that Kidman could receive a one-off prize on November 30 at the annual Evening Standard Drama Awards for her "special and significant contribution to the London theatre."

The ceremony, fortuitously, was on a Monday, the show's dark day on Broadway, which enabled Kidman to make the trans-Atlantic crossing after the previous day's matinee on her private jet.

Among those along for the ride were Glen, Patrick Marber, set designer Mark Thompson, and Caro Newling. "There was a kind of unspoken rule between us that we were not going to even try to be cool" about the experience, says Newling, who, like most of Kidman's guest list, had never flown in a private jet before. "We were going to get horribly excited about everything, and what was so lovely was that Nicole joined in; she was so completely one of us." Having discovered on board that he and Newling shared the same birthday, Thompson, in turn, found himself wrapped up in a cashmere rug courtesy of a solicitous star. "Nicole was very concerned that I have a little sleep."

On Broadway, meanwhile, the fevered box office was tempered somewhat by a largely chilly response to a text whose inherently piecemeal, stop-start structure - shorn of the very specific Donmar environment - shut quite a few critics out of the play. Mendes wasn't wholly surprised, admitting in retrospect that the reputation of the Schnitzler source "isn't that well earned." The director goes on: "*La Ronde* is a disappointing play whenever you see it, since it's essentially the first act of ten plays - a beautiful but bloodless dramatic exercise." Careful not to point an accusing finger at Hare, Mendes argues that the play "really isn't a masterpiece; I think Schnitzler knew it was basically flawed. Indeed, David added a good deal of humanity and romanticism." What then explains the source text's enduring appeal? "It gets to the voyeur in everybody, and the weird thing is that we have become a nation, a world, of voyeurs: at either end of the spectrum, we occupy a fish bowl."

▲ Iain Glen and Nicole Kidman in *The Blue Room*.

Iain Glen felt the play's attraction lay in its treatment of "an area of human behaviour that people are not party to; no one really knows what people get up to privately. That was the frisson within the Donmar: people loved being intimate near two people who were being intimate with each other. And that caused the difficulties we had in America - why, I felt, the play didn't work quite so well. Putting people at the end of a long corridor," as in any big theatre on Broadway or in London, "is very different from having them right there."

Even in Britain, the lingering spell (or not) that was cast by *The Blue Room* varied from person to person: one person's Viagra could be something pointedly bleak and even asexual to another. Mendes points to an "almost Beckettian randomness to the couplings in the play that makes it quite unsexy," coupled with the sense the play conveys in which "people always want to be where they're not; they're not getting what they want, so they move on." In Kidman's view, *The Blue Room*, she says simply, "was a sad play about loneliness." (And about risk, implicitly, as well, with some wondering why more hadn't been made of the threat of AIDS in a contemporary piece exalting the quantity, if not always the quality, of sex.)

Hare as adaptor took a somewhat different view in his desire "to replace that familiar cynical world-weariness associated with being on 'la ronde' with the feeling that 'la ronde' is the only place you can live and grow." To that end, the script became for him "a defence of promiscuity: a celebration of the fact that it is better to be on 'la ronde' than off it. Most plays start warm and end up cold; we wanted to reverse it, starting cold and ending up warm." That, to Hare, was "the basic flip in the story."

A more tangible flip was provided in New York by the proscenium arch of the Cort Theatre, a smallish house by Broadway standards that nonetheless felt too big for *The Blue Room* in every way that mattered, apart, of course, from the increased box office. In New York, says Kidman, "I found the size of the theatre very tough; what's beautiful at the Donmar is that you can absolutely reach out and touch these people." Indeed, there turned out to be a notable irony to the canny tag line coined by Broadway press agent John Barlow - "a play in ten intimate acts" - to describe a New York play that most everyone felt had been far more truly intimate in London.

Nor was the American press as fully in thrall to the event as their London kin had been. While the promise of nudity had clearly spurred sales - "the description of the piece," says Mendes, "was alarming, as if Nicole was frontally naked for ten minutes, parading about" - the titillation fed a scepticism bruisingly put forth by New York Times columnist Frank Rich, a one-time theatre critic at that paper. Dismissing Spencer's Viagra comment as the remark of a British critic "apparently on sabbatical from a monastery," Rich blasted the play's "acute shortfall as both sex show and cultural event." His conclusion: "Anyone in search of pure theatrical Viagra might have had a better shot with the Rockettes."

Hare took Rich's diatribe as part of "a mudslinging campaign from a paper that hates anyone who bypasses the problem of its own power." (By opening to an advance sale of $4 million, *The Blue Room* had rendered the reviews irrelevant - even in the usually omnipotent New York Times.) In the late 1980s Hare and Rich had famously locked horns over director Hare's short-lived Broadway premiere of his own play, *The Secret Rapture*. That shared history aside, Hare, like Mendes, acknowledged that the attack was part of an event that had outpaced its creators, acquiring an all but unstoppable momentum. Its most direct beneficiaries, and rightly so, turned out to be Kidman and Glen, who were on the front line every night communicating a supposedly heartless script to a breathless public. To that extent, Hare records feeling "the New York audience's surprise about halfway through, because the press campaign had represented the play as cold and cynical and unpleasant, and it wasn't any of those things. Instead, there was this play full of rather complicated, interesting feelings." And, Hare maintains, warmth.

Mendes found himself monitoring the New York hubbub from something of a distance, having begun work on *American Beauty*: the film's ultimately Oscar-winning star, Kevin Spacey, showed up on the first day of shooting waving Ben Brantley's frosty review of *The Blue Room* from that day's New York Times. (Brantley had already panned the show in a London roundup, calling the play "a joyless cycle of users and the used.") "I begrudgingly read it," says Mendes, "even though I've never been so determined not to read reviews of a show of mine because I felt it wasn't being looked at in the proper context. There was no sense in which it was ours anymore; it just became a subject for discussion, mostly bitchy. The whole thing was a carnival; it wasn't about the play." To this day, the New York engagement remains probably best documented by Tom Cruise, who was much in evidence making a home video of proceedings. "We were all interviewed," says Hugh Vanstone, deadpan, "to see how difficult the wife was."

For its performers, the Broadway run became about nightly hordes at the stage door, complete with police barricades that are a New York norm and a London anomaly, the likes of Madonna apart. Backstage saw a steady stream of visiting celebrities - Billy Joel, Ron Howard, and Barbara Walters one performance, Gwyneth Paltrow, Goldie Hawn, and Kurt Russell at another. Left for much of the run to their own creative devices, Glen says, "Nic and I did in a way feel abandoned, but it was sort of a nice abandonment. We didn't need to worry about proving ourselves after the play opened; it was just the two of us." The pair shared Christmas with their then-spouses and various children and Mendes also in attendance at the Cruise-Kidman hideaway in the Colorado mountains. While there, Glen's three-year-old son Finlay learned to ski, with each Glen family member given a personal instructor.

The Broadway *Blue Room* finished prematurely February 25, 1999, after its eighty-first performance - the engagement cut short twelve days early due to a virulent throat infection that ended up felling Kidman. That same night had been scheduled as a gala fundraiser for the Donmar back home, with Glen and Kidman expected at a post-show bash at which an ailing Kidman never appeared. (The event nonetheless raised £85,000 for the theatre.) "It was humiliating and surreal," says Kidman, who - like Natasha Richardson in Mendes' Broadway *Cabaret* (though for different reasons) - never got the closure that comes with finishing a triumphant theatre run. But by that point Kidman had already been cast in *Moulin Rouge* and knew she would be singing on screen, so guarding her voice was doubly crucial. Glen and Kidman in any case continued their friendship well after the end of the production, with the actor among those at Kidman's Millennium Eve boat party in Sydney.

Of the play's initial creative team, Kidman undoubtedly benefitted most directly from *The Blue Room*, though Hare would have the satisfaction of seeing the play quickly revived by director Loveday Ingram, first at Chichester and then in the West End, as well as frequently produced abroad. (David Leveaux directed its Japanese premiere, while the Paris version saved its celebrity draw for the male lead, the ubiquitous Daniel Auteuil.) Glen would segue exactly four years later to co-starring at the National in *A Streetcar Named Desire* opposite yet another London theatre first-timer, Glenn Close. By that point, the actor had presumably been deemed a good bet when it came to providing a solid and gracious anchor to visiting stars. At the same time, the pecs needed to follow in *Streetcar* where Marlon Brando has so formidably led remain one legacy of Glen's *Blue Room* run in New York, where the performer's sleek if undeveloped physique got bulked up at the gym as is that city's showbiz norm. Hare laughs, as he recalls admonishing Glen in London to get his bodily act together for New York. "I'd say to Iain, 'You can't be a serious leading man on Broadway with those pectorals.' Finally, all that work has paid off."

Whatever their ongoing puzzlements about that entire period, Kidman's collaborators point to her as the very real heroine of *The Blue Room*'s not always pleasant elevation from mere production to verifiable phenomenon. "I feel like for Nicole it was a very special time," says Sam Mendes, citing the play as "the moment she became an entity quite separate from Tom [Cruise] - and I'm sure she was aware that was happening. It just turned people around to her and surprised them, and I'm very proud *The Blue Room* did that for her." Lucy Davies, who was by Mendes' right arm for much of the London run, concurs. "I know Tom used to say that to Sam all the time: 'Thank you, you've made her.' Of course, film actors never hear the audience applauding, so that must have been an extraordinary experience for her. She did work so hard."

"Nicole was bloody good," says David Hare, who was keen to disavow any responsibility for the subsequent - and seemingly ceaseless - spiral of celebrity casting of which *The Blue Room* was such a momentous part. (Hare has done his bit by vetoing some pretty ludicrous casting ideas for the play.) "If the idea of what we did has been ripped off by people a thousand times less talented than Nicole, that's not our fault. Our production featured the best actress in the world for that particular role."

Hare uses the experience when wanting to prove to doubtful actors the ways in which a play can kickstart a film career, as *The Blue Room* did for Kidman. (And as Mendes' *Cabaret* had more modestly done for Alan Cumming.) It was very specifically on the back of Hare's play that Kidman got both *Moulin Rouge* and *The Hours*. Baz Luhrmann hired her for the former after attending the play's first Broadway preview, while director Stephen Daldry cast her as Virginia Woolf in the latter, adapted as it happens by Hare from Michael Cunningham's novel, after admiring her stage turn as the Actress.

"It's amazing how little things lead to bigger things," says Kidman. "I basically credit Sam with the last few years of my career. *The Blue Room* changed my life."

to illyria and 'beyond'

chapter 7

What, then, for an encore? Having got *The Blue Room* on its feet on Broadway, Sam Mendes fulfilled a date with destiny that had seemed a long time coming - his first movie.

Mendes had been cautious in approaching film, and the film world, passing up various projects over time: among them, *The Wings of the Dove*, the screen adaptation of *Little Voice*, even a job high up at Channel 4. That last option, Mendes recalls, was appealing by way of contrast with the economic climate he was used to on the British stage. "Who wouldn't want to have £32 million a year to invest in all the right things - directors, writers, artists - and not have to scrape and beg and save like you do in the British theatre just to keep your building open, let alone do good work?" The sums available in film were clearly on a different scale from an enterprise like the Donmar, which not long before had been enormously pleased to receive £185,000 from the Broadway producers Barry and Fran Weissler. The husband-and-wife team behind the smash revival of *Chicago* on Broadway, the Weisslers bought out the Donmar, which had been planning a separate revival of the same musical, so that the Broadway version could be replicated on the West End. The American money, notes Mendes, "paid for *The Front Page*. Barry and Fran were impeccably behaved and on time and fantastic."

It wasn't long into Mendes' regime before film scripts began to be floated as very real options - *Mushroom Soup*, by the journalist and critic Patrick Marmion, and *Morality Play*, an adaptation of the historical novel by Barry Unsworth, which Mendes had read in galleys. But as far back as 1995 and *Company*, Mendes was well aware, he says, that "in the next two to three years there would be an opportunity to direct a first movie, (whereas) the Donmar will not always be here." How appropriate, then, that his film directing debut came with an American script written by a playwright (Alan Ball) and starring two theatre-trained actors (Kevin Spacey and Annette Bening). What's more, says Mendes, "the back wall of the Donmar was in every shot of *American Beauty*," sometimes almost literally so: more than one shot in the movie frames the actors in ways recognizable to Donmar regulars accustomed to a theatrical backdrop that, over the Mendes decade, has built up thirty-five layers of paint.

In practical terms, *American Beauty* raised a question put forward again two years later by *Road To Perdition*: Mendes' absence from the theatre to which he was still attached. On the one hand, of course, his freelance activities had all along fed the Donmar . "My way here has always been to go away and bring those relationships back into the building, and if I hadn't been doing that, Nicole wouldn't have come to do *The Blue Room*, Alan wouldn't have come to do *Cabaret*, Adrian Lester would never have come to do

Company." And it wasn't as if Mendes had never before been employed elsewhere - his National Theatre productions of *The Birthday Party* and *Othello* both opened during his Donmar tenure, while his West End *Oliver!* was followed back at home base by *The Glass Menagerie* and *Company*, which came as a welcome relief: "I was flying then because I was completely free, having been part of a huge machine [with *Oliver!*]." Then there was the Off-Broadway workshop of a new Sondheim musical, *Wise Guys*: the project was aborted at the end of its limited run and has since changed titles (to *Gold!*) and directors (to Harold Prince).

❝I'd seen some stuff there over the years - *Poppie Nongena* from South Africa and a little later the Cheek By Jowl *Midsummer Night's Dream*. And I have always liked spaces like that, so in a way it's almost the ideal theatre for me. It feels like fringe - like you're performing in a living room - and you can think your stuff out there; you don't have to rely on tremendous artifice in terms of voice and gesture. As a result, you sense the personality of an audience very quickly there. And you're right bang in the middle of town, so you feel as if you're in the middle of things.

It's so small, the Donmar, and because it's always going for limited runs, it creates such a buzz when the play is inaccessible. There's that little room that 250 people a night can get into or not, and if it's something people want to see, for every 250 who can get in there are 800 others who can't. There's a sense of event about the theatre because of the limited accessibility of the place which just stokes up its sex appeal. On the other hand, that's partly what theatre is all about: being present at something that's going to come out of the air and disappear back into the air forever.

The Donmar is a great theatre. I'm glad I got to perform there and that I qualify as one of their alumni. ❞

COLIN FIRTH, actor
Three Days of Rain, 1999

Wherever he was, Mendes made sure to be available at the end of a phone. Caro Newling recalls ringing up to discuss some aspect of the spring, 2002, London premiere of *Lobby Hero* while Mendes was in the wintry American midwest filming *Road To Perdition*. "Sam said, 'I'm standing on the edge of a lake waiting for the sun to come up with four thousand extras,' and I was saying, 'Right, never mind that. Now what about...'" Newling laughs. "Sam can have these conversations in the middle of nowhere surrounded by thousands of people under intense pressure to deliver the day's filming, and he just gets it; it's an extraordinary global view, it really is, and that's a great artistic director." By contrast, says Newling, "I'm the opposite: I can only see what is in front of me, so we're quite a good combination. I'm very, very dogged."

Even in Hollywood, Mendes was casting his mind towards the Donmar and towards an environment where different worlds could be created via the imagination as opposed to literal reproduction. "Let me tell you, when you've worked on one piece of work for eighteen months to two years on a set with one hundred and fifty people and thousands of extras and an enormous amount of pressure and an enormous distance between the word and the end product, there's a real desire to get back in the rehearsal room where the word and the end product are the same thing: instantaneous, boom, it's a performance." By way of illustration, says Mendes, in the theatre "you say you're in the Arctic, and you're in the Arctic; you don't have to shoot the fucking Arctic or go there with three hundred other people and seven juggernauts in order to say you're in the Arctic." So it wasn't surprising to find Mendes back at the Donmar within a week of winning his Oscar to announce his next production - a World War I drama that placed a mostly male cast adrift, literally and metaphysically, in a French forest.

To the Green Fields Beyond opened September 25, 2000, nearly two years exactly from the Donmar debut of *The Blue Room.* But Nick Whitby's quiet analysis of the workings of a British tank corps wasn't the director's first choice to fill the slot. That had been nothing less than *Twelfth Night.* But under the theory that one could always return to Shakespeare's comedy, a new play by a young living writer merited attention. And so Mendes responded to Whitby's script when it was sent to him by Sebastian Born, who is the agent for both men. The National had also been considering the play, but Mendes read it and decided to do it the same afternoon. As a way back into the theatre, Mendes had been looking for just such a delicate piece. "I didn't want to do something that said, 'Look at me.' I have never treated the theatre like that, and I don't intend to." But if Mendes was keen to ease himself once more into the milieu from which he had come, the profile that went with winning an Oscar posed its own challenges.

On the one hand, there were the rehearsals. The *Green Fields* ensemble, headed by Dougray Scott and Ray Winstone, "was a difficult company to unite," says Mendes. "Everyone had different ways of doing things, and none of them were wrong. It took every ounce of what stagecraft I had to create something that seemed utterly organic," especially since Anthony Ward's shimmering birch-filled set crammed thirty-five trees into a three-sided space. ("Everybody had trees to look through," says Ward, "not just the people on the sides.") More disconcerting, however, was the feeling that Mendes, post-Oscar, was being looked at anew, not least when it emerged halfway through rehearsal that he was planning a second film, this one to star Tom Hanks. "I would be lying if I felt that some of the actors weren't thinking, 'I wonder if I have a part in that movie,' and that's not helpful in a rehearsal room because you want people to impress you with the play, not themselves; it wasn't freeing as a rehearsal experience." On the other hand, Mendes' greater renown had become, in box office terms, the theatre's own best ambassador, helping generate over £50,000 at a *Green Fields* gala performance on October 17.

The reviews inevitably focused more on Mendes than the play, with various critics apparently put out that the director had dared to forego *Twelfth Night* for this. "People reviewed the play as a career decision and couldn't see the play at all," says Mendes, who remains "astonished" by a reaction that he calls "extremely unfortunate for an extremely talented writer. It was as if they blamed Nick [Whitby] for dragging me away from the *Twelfth Night* they would like to have seen, again as if," he smiles wryly, "*Twelfth Night* were going to go away." In terms of its low-key and deliberate accretion of emotion, *Green Fields*, says Mendes, "was a kind of cousin to *Translations.*" And by a happy turn of events, one of its defining performances came from Finbar Lynch, formerly of *Translations*, here playing the agitated pragmatist of an army corps clearly facing collective extinction. "I just felt for Sam," Lynch says of Mendes. "He was regrounding himself, if you like. He knew people were gunning for him, and he knew that at some point people were going to dance gleefully on his grave." The run itself was not without incident: nine performances - the most for any Donmar play - were lost to colds and infections and to an eye injury that befell Winstone. At one point, author Whitby went on in a smallish role while company member Gary Powell was promoted up to Winstone's part. But any offstage concerns paled next to the visible teamwork of a company embarked upon one of the Donmar's more mysterious and teasing plays: a report from the road to oblivion, told as if from the inside.

Mendes before long was off to America again, this time bringing to the screen in *Road To Perdition* the sepia-hued world of Chicago mobsters during the 1930s. Other theatres might not so easily have done without their leader. But, says Caro Newling, "this was never a regime where, if Sam wasn't there, the thing came to a grinding halt. [The Donmar] was set up so it wasn't hanging on Sam's every word." Newling quickly recognised that film had its own exigencies. "In a way, Sam's going into movies was different because it was a world we couldn't play a role in." But even at his busiest, says Newling, "Sam never lost sight of the detail of the Donmar." Mendes, in turn, was fully aware of his home theatre, even on Oscar night (when Rachael Stirling, Ron Cook, and Helen McCrory were among the Donmar players gathered in the basement of One Aldwych at an all-night party to cheer Mendes on). Amid the ever-increasing limelight, Mendes found himself "bobbing around in a shipwreck reaching for the bits of driftwood I know, and the Donmar, believe me, was the biggest and most comforting bit of driftwood. It is such a great leveller and was such a great leveller for me." His affiliation with DreamWorks SKG, the Hollywood studio behind *American Beauty*, meant a palpable gain back in England: DreamWorks money enabled Mendes to set up a Donmar Films office in Neal Street directly underneath the theatre's administrative home. In addition, the theatre would receive £100,000 per annum from DreamWorks, with the proviso that any other studio that might employ Mendes would take over the financial responsibilities of the deal at that time.

> **❝**I did a play recently somewhere else where the stage management gave off that they were bored in the rehearsal room and just weren't into the play, and that would never ever happen at the Donmar. Maybe that's because people feel they are in a place where good theatre is happening and where good directors are working. And maybe that's not always the case.
> Everyone at the Donmar is committed to the theatre and to what is going on there, and that has to come from Sam. And then you've got Caro and Anne - people that have been there a long time - and it's a cliché to say it's like a family. But it is a very close working group, and I think they're very good at making you feel that you are part of a community.**❞**

FINBAR LYNCH, actor
Translations, 1993
Fool For Love, 1996
To the Green Fields Beyond, 2000

On the artistic front it was business as usual at a theatre that was doing more of what it had always done and, in some cases, arguably better. The Donmar for several years had employed artistic associates - first John Crowley, then David Leveaux and Michael Grandage - to allow for continuity while still giving new talent a foot in the door. It was in April 2001, with Mendes preparing *Road To Perdition*, that Crowley came into his own on *Tales From Hollywood*, another first revival of a modern play. At the National in 1983, Peter Gill had sent Christopher Hampton's script careering across the vast Olivier, as if the thrust stage of that auditorium were itself the vast terrain covered by a play about European émigrés to Hollywood. Eighteen years later, aided by a swimming pool set from American designer Scott Pask that showed an unusually cunning command of the dictates of the Donmar, Crowley turned a putative epic into a mournful dreamplay. "The space effortlessly responded to the fluidity I wanted the production to have," says Crowley of a staging that represents "the sum of everything I know about how Donmar works." And

Anthony Ward's tree-filled set - 35 birches in all - for *To the Green Fields Beyond* ▶

although Hampton's focus in on the play was on the walking dead, including a narrator speaking from beyond the grave, *Tales From Hollywood* wasn't without its own spry wit: "Force of habit," quipped Phil Davis' Bertolt Brecht, whose every appearance was accompanied by the raising of the house lights. The only downside to a happy occasion - the revival was Crowley's favourite of his five Donmar productions to that point - was box office attendance of 76%, the second lowest of that season. (*A Lie of the Mind*, the Shepard revival immediately following, played to 60%.)

The same year saw another Donmar associate, Michael Grandage, back again and collaborating once more with Peter Nichols, this time on a revival of *Privates On Parade* that turned what could have been an exercise in camp into its own meditation on exile: a dissection in song and dance of the English psyche abroad - specifically the Far East in 1948. A largely autobiographical account of Nichols' own experiences in Malaya as a member of the Combined Services Entertainment, *Privates* bears all the hallmarks of a flat-out romp: not every show has the, uh, balls to send up Carmen Miranda, Marlene Dietrich, and Noel Coward. Grandage's achievement was to offer up the full pastiche of Denis King's score alongside an undertow of pain to do with the cost of sustaining a stiff upper lip - or not, as the case may be. "I think being in that space," recalls leading man Roger Allam, who played Terri Dennis, the military man as outrageous queen, "we were able to get back to the play," rather than the series of turns

Sam Mendes' debut film, *American Beauty*, found numerous visual echoes of the Donmar's much-vaunted back wall, not least in a defining encounter between Wes Bentley and Kevin Spacey. ▼ The point is illustrated here by the sets for *The Blue Room* and *Design For Living* (with Clive Owen, Rachel Weisz and Paul Rhys) ▶

that a more lazily directed *Privates* can become. For its second London revival since the show's 1977 Royal Shakespeare Company premiere (a "very dull" Tony Slattery, reports Nichols, was Terri in a production at Greenwich), the nudity was played down. The unexpected result: "The one or two flashes we did have got more objections this time than we ever had [the first time round]. There are not all that many privates on parade, and there were even less in Michael's production." Backstage, as had been true of *To the Green Fields Beyond*, the men were apportioned across the two dressing rooms, the rowdier performers in one, those who were "slightly more sedate," says Allam, in the other. (He and co-star Malcolm Sinclair, inheriting Nigel Hawthorne's original role as Giles Flack, an army major determinedly strait-laced and straight, plumped for the latter.) The production's lone woman, Indira Varma, put herself in with the quieter lot, declining the offer of a protective curtain - in keeping, no doubt, with the full-frontal spirit of the piece.

66 It's a very nice space, actually, to play in: a very intimate space, though it isn't easy with the stage on three sides and a very high balcony. But given that stricture, they do wonders with it: a bit like the Almeida, you can turn the Donmar into anything you want. Also, the immediacy actually puts you on your spot. You can't hide anywhere; you're just there, and you have to do it. And what you get is involvement - as an audience member, you're very much a participator in what's going on, and I think that's a great plus. The whole experience of the Donmar has a very democratic feel to it, which is actually how theatre should work. If you're doing a piece like *The Little Foxes* that requires ensemble acting, it plays into its favour if you are all together and not distanced in any way. I would choose to work at the Donmar a lot. It attracts an audience engaged in the theatre that doesn't just go to see the big things. They're interested in acting and interested in writers and interested in the play. 99

PENELOPE WILTON, actress
Three By Harold Pinter, 1998
The Little Foxes, 2001

Privates further confirmed Grandage's skill with actors in a show that equally fielded smutty double entendres ("you can't judge a sausage by its foreskin") and subtextual pathos. Taking the audience-grabbing part for which Kenneth Branagh had early on been mooted, Roger Allam enjoyed trying out yet another physical transformation on William, his two-year-old son. "During his time on this planet, I've gone through so many different appearances" - with a beard one part, without it the next, not to mention making himself up to look like Hitler for the National production of *Albert Speer* - that the shaved body and dyed blonde hair necessary for Terri Dennis never phased the boy. William, says his father, "seemed to accept it with good grace." Grandage, in turn, "loved the idea that Roger went home and shaved his legs while feeding his young son." In the end, the actor's commitment paid off. Allam, "a wonderful man of the theatre" in Grandage's view, won an Olivier for the performance. And the show, budgeted at 75% across the run, played to 92%.

The ever-so-English *Privates* was immediately preceded by a contrastingly buttoned-up American drama, Lillian Hellman's *The Little Foxes*. This time, however, the director was a newcomer to the Donmar: Marianne Elliott, daughter of Michael Elliott, himself a director who had been best known for

Scott Pask's amazingly clever swimming pool set for *Tales From Hollywood*, starring Ben Daniels ▶

his pioneering work at the Royal Exchange, Manchester. Hellman's warhorse had certainly proven itself over time. Bette Davis played the ruthless Regina Giddens in William Wyler's 1941 film, with Fay Compton and Elizabeth Taylor taking the same role in the West End in 1942 and 1982, respectively. At the Donmar, it was Penelope Wilton's turn to play the only sister in a family of scheming Hubbard brothers who makes it a point of survival to give as good as she gets. And while the Elizabeth Taylor version had turned the Hellman original into a melodramatic travesty of itself, Elliott and Wilton succeeded by playing the text absolutely straight - and releasing, in the process, a pent-up emotion of nearly Ibsenesque power. (Elliott must have come by her skill genetically, since her father had shown a particular gift for Strindberg and Ibsen.)

In Wilton's view, the task was about "not seeing Regina as a two-dimensional person. It is difficult to let your husband die on stage while you sit there and not have it become farcical; we had to find a way of doing that - of finding the truth in that." One way of doing so was to expose Regina's essential loneliness, a sense of separation that was only intensified by the near-constant physical presence of her family. It helped that Elliott had taken her leading lady the previous August on a two-week research trip to New Orleans in order to investigate the American South first hand. "The heat was so vivid," says Elliott, "it really powered your imagination." So did a Lez Brotherston set that painted the Donmar back wall a looming grey, with the words Hubbard and Sons sprayed upon it. And having worked so extensively up at the Royal Exchange herself, Marianne Elliott felt at home with the nearly comparable three-quarter configuration of the Donmar. "We took on certain rules from the round, so that Penelope never ever faced straight out." As a result, adds Elliott, "you could never quite see Regina's full face": a potentially blunt, brash play emerged as newly brooding and morally complex.

Mendes wasn't much in evidence during *The Little Foxes.* "Sam seemed to be never there when I was," says Wilton, who first worked at the Donmar in 1998 in Harold Pinter's *A Kind of Alaska.* But though he was otherwise occupied in post-production on his second film, he was still available for consultation, much to Elliott's delight. One of the crucial parts in the play is that of Regina's alcoholic sister-in-law Birdie, and Elliott needed another director with whom to confer on casting. The list of options had narrowed down to Brid

> **I'd seen the odd show at the Donmar before Sam took it over and had absolutely hated the seating. It always seemed a very difficult space. As an audience member, you have this funny, angular relationship to the stage. But everybody's so wonderful there - Caro and Anne, along with Sam - that one is always made to feel so much part of something. In some ways, that's why one fantasizes that one has worked there much more than one has done: it's one of the important theatres in London, along with the Almeida, as a serious alternative to the National and the RSC. That's why, whatever problems there are with it, one always feels positive about working there: you're positive about the space even though it drives you mad.**
> **In the early days, all the talk was about Sam's youth, and we had all these jokes about our age differences. But Sam is such that you don't even sort of question it, really. It's not that he's a rollercoaster or steamroller; in fact, he's very easy.**

ANTHONY WARD, designer
Assassins, 1992
Nine, 1996
To the Green Fields Beyond, 2000
Uncle Vanya (sets), 2002
Twelfth Night (sets), 2002

Brennan, the Irish actress whom Mendes had seen on his first trip to New York in *Dancing At Lughnasa*, for which she won a Tony. Despite being occupied in the editing suite on *Road To Perdition*, Mendes took time to trade thoughts. "Sam knew Brid very well," says Elliott, "and we had a great conversation on the phone. That's what a good artistic director can do: just empower you, give you confidence."

And know when to bow out.

That crucial decision began to be made late in 2000 during the annual lunch at which, says Mendes, he and Caro Newling would discuss "every year, once a year, what absolute reason we had to be running this building. If you don't discuss that, you don't renew your enthusiasm, and you just assume the theatre is going to be there." The tenth-anniversary season was approaching. With it would come the announcement that this was to be Mendes' final year. "Doesn't this seem like the right time to go?" Mendes remembers asking Newling. "And I was fairly certain that it was." Ten seemed an appropriate number of years to have done the job, especially since - on the topic of numbers - things were looking up.

Prior to the arrival of Rachel Weinstein, for instance, the theatre had four hundred "friends" (i.e. donors) contributing £13,500 between them; four-and-a-half years later, the Donmar could point to over two thousand supporters, an American division included, bringing in more than £350,000 a year. An ongoing "first look" deal with New York producer Anita Waxman - inaugurated in July, 1999 - was providing the theatre £220,000 a year: in return, Waxman got first dibs on any commercial future for a Donmar show (and, as a result, led the trail of producers to the podium in June, 2000, when *The Real Thing* won its Tony Award for Best Revival of a Play.) The sum, agreed for an initial period of three years, made up for the collapse, also in 1999, of Warehouse Productions, the Donmar's abortive commercial wing. Conceived as a parallel commercial company to the Donmar, Warehouse Productions had been formed in 1998 with the intention of producing three shows over eighteen months straight into the West End. The line-up began promisingly with a double-bill of *The Real Inspector Hound* and *Black Comedy*, directed by Gregory Doran, that did well enough to recast and also tour. But Warehouse Productions lost steam with an overly decorative, emotionally underpowered revival of Tennessee Williams's *Suddenly Last Summer* from Sean Mathias that closed early. That was followed by a disastrously attended (and reviewed) Old Vic revival of *Antigone*, starring Tara Fitzgerald and directed by Declan Donnellan. Among those not altogether surprised by the failure of Warehouse Productions was former Donmar board member Nica Burns. "If you're going to run a theatre like the Donmar, you shouldn't ever think of anything beyond the productions for the Donmar," says Burns, who had been reluctant to voice her scepticism at the

> 66 You can look through their ten year history at the theatre and see very clearly that Sam and Caro - cruel though it sometimes is - do give you one chance, and actually it's called, I'm afraid, being a grown-up producer. The Donmar is a deceptive space - it's not an easy space, I don't think. There are not a lot of choices about where you can stand on that stage and be able to be seen by everybody. If you come too far downstage, you go out of view upstage. And the profession is clearly aesthetically divided between people who see the back wall as an obstacle or as something you can use. If you've got it, you should use it, I say; it's a beautiful gift. 99

MICHAEL GRANDAGE, director
Good, 1999
Passion Play, 2000
Merrily We Roll Along, 2000
Privates On Parade, 2001

time. "People have to discover things for themselves; I didn't think it was right to be the wet blanket."

Nonetheless, there was no doubt that the theatre had by now become sufficiently valued and known not to confront - as it had in April, 1996 - the risk of near-closure. Throughout the 1990s, the Donmar had walked a perilous financial path, welcoming in sponsors (the Evening Standard, the Daily Telegraph, Covent Garden Estates) even as other sources of revenue fell away: Mercury, for instance, whose crucial early support dried up almost immediately when the company was taken over by Cable and Wireless. Another blow came early in 1997 when it was confirmed that the Donmar would not get to participate in a National Lottery Stabilisation Pilot Scheme, thereby negating a possible £250,000 from that particular source. It took the combination of the Arts Council appraisal in 1998, *The Blue Room*, the arrival of Rachel Weinstein, and Mendes' own widening reach to shift the Donmar's position to one where the theatre could in an internal document itself speak of planning the 2000-2001 season "with relative security when compared with the uncertainty of previous [years]."

On the one hand, Mendes was absolutely right to argue in a letter to the Prime Minister late in 1998 the iniquities of a funding process that saw the Donmar's grant increase, he wrote, "by a mere £10,000" - to £160,000, less than half the sum then received by the Almeida, the Hampstead, and others - "while our friends round the corner at the Royal Opera House receive an additional £12.8 million." In October 2001, a new principal sponsor was well established in the form of the global software company SAP, which committed itself to providing £500,000 over three years, having first dipped into the Donmar as a one-off sponsor of *Merrily We Roll Along* the previous Christmas. By April 2002, SAP and other multiple sources of funding had led the Donmar board to project reserves of £860,000 by the end of the financial year 2003. The board's chair, Martin McCallum, points out that the Donmar had learned the lesson of not "putting all our eggs in one basket, or even two," whether they be Roger Wingate or Mercury, however welcome and essential those outlays were. The anticipated reserve, some £300,000 better than forecast, was a testament to hard work and tenacity at a time when, it was agreed, no one could afford to

> " Everyone who works in that building is honed only to their craft. There's none of this thing of the lighting guy telling you he's also writing plays and authors telling you they are also wanting to act: everyone there respects the essential skill, and it is done with such generosity, honesty, and clarity of thought.
> I remember on the first preview of *In A Little World Of Our Own* suddenly realising that the theatre has height. It's quite deceptive on stage when you walk on because it seems very very intimate. There is an immediacy with the audience that any Donmar performer always has to be aware of. It's not a place that makes you lazy. The Donmar is an extremely creative place and a very safe place to fail. That's why, I think, they take risks. "

HELEN McCRORY, actress
In a Little World of Our Own (visiting), 1998
How I Learned To Drive, 1998
Uncle Vanya, 2002
Twelfth Night, 2002

Olivier Award-winner Roger Allam (centre) with (clockwise from top) Justin Salinger, Nigel Harman, Hugh Sachs and Daniel Tuite in *Privates On Parade* ▶

▲ SAP sponsors Hans-Peter Klaey and Peter Robertshaw
flank the Donmar trio of Caro Newling,
Rachel Weinstein, and Michael Grandage

be complacent: apparent economic victory, however sweet, was equally fragile.

The numbers also showed the way in which it sometimes pays to be ambitious - as Mendes and Newling were determined to be in programming their final year. (Newling had announced that she would similarly vacate her Donmar post, joining Mendes in a new commercial enterprise after seeing the theatre's follow-up artistic director into the job.) And having begun ten years previously with a bold American premiere, the pair were to bow out by doing the same again, yet bolder. The plan was to mount five American plays (among them, two world premieres, Keith Reddin's *Frame 312*, the decided low point of the season, included) in a sequence of work to be underwritten by £275,000 in sponsorship. That series would be followed by a repertory engagement of Shakespeare and Chekhov, directed by Mendes and jointly performed by one ensemble over the sort of lengthy rehearsal period more common to the National. For his farewell, the director was at last turning to *Twelfth Night*, to be produced alongside Brian Friel's version of *Uncle Vanya*. After all, it was while awaiting the reviews thirteen years before of *The Cherry Orchard* that Mendes had come upon a then-abandoned theatre. What goes around comes around.

The 2002 American season wasn't the Donmar's first such line-up: in the Carlton-sponsored new writing season three years previously, Lucy Davies had programmed a trio of plays billed collectively as "American Imports." Of those, the best received was the only Donmar production to return for an encore engagement - Richard Greenberg's generational drama *Three Days of Rain*, a play virtually defined by the very irony that American writing is believed not to possess. Its structure is vaguely Stoppardian: siblings in 1995 in the first act play their own parents in the second act. Robin Lefevre's production marked the sole appearance to date at the Donmar of one of the theatre's fondest alumni, Colin Firth. His affection for the space notwithstanding, Firth learned firsthand on opening night the pitfalls of appearing in a venue without a stage door. Keen to get some air before the performance, he exited in costume through the fire escape door only to find himself on the street, locked out. The only solution was to re-enter through the foyer, in the process, says Firth, "probably curtly dismissing people asking for autographs because I was due on stage in twenty minutes for the first time in six years." Amid what was overall "a wonderful experience," that particular incident was a bad one. "The only down side to the Donmar is that the backstage escape facility is not great."

Greenberg never saw *Three Days of Rain* but was able to make it to London for *Take Me Out*, which was the last of the five American plays to be produced in 2002. Of the preceding ones, two moved directly

American Imports 2002: Daniel Sunjata (top) in *Take Me Out* and David Tennant in *Lobby Hero* ▶

❝ It was very exciting at the Donmar, just the thought that you could be in that space behaving in a human way and having people see it and understand what you were doing. If you're used to working in the cinema and being internal and having a slight expression convey a ton of emotion, the Donmar makes a nice way to bridge the gap between cinema acting and the stage; it's a very cinematic space. Everybody who works there was fantastic, from the people at the box office to Sam on down - they were really kind, good people, and it was such a good place to work. People said, 'Oh, the Donmar, you're going to have the best experience.' I was sure I'd love it but I really had no idea what to expect. What I found is, it really is magical. **❞**

GWYNETH PALTROW, actress
Proof, 2002

into the West End: Stephen Adly Guirgis' *Jesus Hopped the 'A' Train*, directed (as it had been Off-Broadway) by the actor Philip Seymour Hoffman, and Kenneth Lonergan's *Lobby Hero*, a droll morality play whose commercial transfer closed a week early: a peculiar ad campaign pitching Lonergan's Arthur Miller-like text as some kind of cartoon cannot have helped its cause. At the Donmar, both plays had performed above expectation - to 91% and 85%, respectively. So did *Take Me Out*, whose setting in the world of baseball didn't bother a London audience that could always consult a programme glossary to find out the meaning of the word "pitcher." "This isn't New Writing Lite," Mendes had said of the American play sweep, and *Take Me Out* most emphatically was not. After all, rare is the play that can spiral out from the towel-snapping world of locker-room banter (and the attendant nudity) to tackle issues of sexuality, racism and even the components of democracy. And yet, for sheer buzz, none of the American plays could compare to *Take Me Out*'s predecessor in the series, *Proof*, and not simply because David Auburn's Broadway hit had already won a Pulitzer and a Tony during a long New York run. (In London, such accolades can act as a deterrent, as *How I Learned To Drive* had shown.) The self-evident enticement on this occasion was the first Donmar production since *The Blue Room* to feature a bona fide film star: Gwyneth Paltrow.

From the outset, Caro Newling was worried that the presence of an Oscar-winning American performer might give off the wrong signals, even if Paltrow's colleagues in the play (Ronald Pickup, Richard Coyle, Sara Stewart) were all accomplished London theatre folk. Complicating matters was the fact that *Proof*'s director, John Madden, had been tapped by Miramax to direct a film of that very play. And since Madden and Paltrow had collaborated successfully on *Shakespeare In Love*, how could *Proof* not look like some kind of dry run for an eventual movie? Especially since Miramax co-chairman Harvey Weinstein could be heard on his mobile phone at the press night interval more or less announcing as much.

In the end, such concerns didn't matter to the critics, who adored Paltrow if not necessarily the play, notwithstanding Madden's almost Chekhovian approach to the text. (The resistance to Auburn's script, which was curtly dismissed by some as a kind of downmarket American dilution of *Copenhagen*, was both myopic and ironic: Auburn first began working on the play while in fact living in Holloway, north London, in 1998.) In any case, a city apparently in need of a new 'It Girl' seemed, however briefly, to have found her. The adulatory reaction to seeing on stage an American actress who had made many a film in

Richard Coyle and Gwyneth Paltrow in rehearsal for Proof ▶

London chimed in with British press coverage which, Kidman-style, attempted to chronicle Paltrow's every move: a scowl at unwanted photographers one minute, her supposed purchase of a £1.25 million Chelsea home the next. Of particular interest was the concurrent appearance on London stages of Paltrow and her good friend, Madonna, who was busy down the road at Wyndham's in *Up For Grabs* eliciting reviews every bit as bad as Paltrow's had been good. (Both, it seems, were equally loyal, finding time amid busy schedules to see one another's shows.)

The prospect of any film of *Proof*, to be fair, seemed far from the minds of its star or director, who were jointly focused instead on the assignment at hand. Madden had last directed on the London stage at the National in 1981 before decamping to theatre work in America and then to TV and, latterly, film back in the UK. Paltrow, the daughter of the veteran Broadway performer Blythe Danner, had never appeared on stage in her home city of New York. Her theatre CV, too, was limited to a summer theatre festival in the northwest corner of Massachusetts, where she had over the years played Shakespeare's Rosalind in *As You Like It* and Chekhov's Nina in *The Seagull*, with her mother as Arkadina. It was his knowledge of Paltrow on screen that led Madden to encourage her back to the theatre: "I felt Gwyneth would just gain such a huge amount from the process of feeling the work she was doing validated moment by moment by the audience."

Paltrow, in turn, was game for an experience that began with her rehearsing on the Kilburn High Road for £350 a week, her macrobiotic diet the delight of a company that found itself sharing in the meals served up by the actress's two chefs (one for savoury dishes, the other for sweets). "For me," Paltrow says of the offer to do the play, "it was fantastic: the idea of working in a space that was that intimate, especially with a contemporary piece where you can take risks." As Kidman had before her, Paltrow early in rehearsals was put through her vocal paces by Patsy Rodenburg. But whereas Kidman needed to develop five different stage voices for David Hare's play, Rodenburg's task this time round, she says, was about "turning Gwyneth's attention towards listening": an important component to the production, since Paltrow was playing a withdrawn Illinois depressive who has inherited her late father's gift for maths - and, more than likely, his mental instability. Was the relative theatre neophyte a good student? Rodenburg gave her report. "I think Gwyneth was very frightened, but you never saw it on the surface. She's very contained and very professional, and she's got superb instincts."

Paltrow's staying power wasn't bad, either, as became clear early in the evening performance on May 18, three days after opening night. While reaching for a notebook in the first scene, the actress fell over a chair and into a table, severely dislocating her left knee. Quite literally hobbling her way through the rest of the show, Paltrow went on Sunday (luckily, her day off) to see an orthopaedic consultant at the Wellington Hospital. His diagnosis called for rest, but Paltrow wouldn't have it. "Even thinking about it

▲ Sam Mendes (centre) surrounded by the ensemble of *Uncle Vanya* and *Twelfth Night*, his final two productions as artistic director

sends me through the roof in pain," says Paltrow, speaking five weeks after the incident. But abandoning a production without understudies just wasn't an option. Julia Christie can quote the conversation she had with the actress, who arrived on the Monday limping, her knee in a brace: "The doctor said I should have the next five weeks off," Paltrow informed Christie. "I've told them, 'no way.'"

Paltrow's persistence resulted in a closing night performance June 15 that far surpassed the press night: not only had her voice got stronger (and less nasal) but so had her access to the fraught emotions of a heroine who comes almost to fear her own genius. The sellout house responded with a standing ovation that seemed to have less to do with the celebrity quotient than with honouring genuinely accomplished work. (Anyone who had seen the separate Broadway production of *Proof* would have been equally impressed by Coyle and Stewart, who were at least the match of their roles' originators in New York.) An emotional Paltrow took three bows before departing the stage with an endearingly shy wave to the house. Afterwards, she repaired along with the cast and other friends to a Soho karaoke bar. Sara Stewart, who shared a dressing room with the star for five weeks, was left with the memory of a festive Paltrow singing "Bootylicious," the chart-topping song from Destiny's Child.

July 1, 2002: Gwyneth Paltrow has been in the papers doing the fashionista rounds in Paris, while Nicole Kidman has just arrived in Romania to begin a six-month shoot on *Cold Mountain*.

An alternate scenario might have found Kidman upstairs in the rehearsal rooms above the Old Vic, helping herself to biscuits and Nescafé. That's where Mendes has gathered the company for the first day of rehearsals on his final project, the Chekhov-Shakespeare pairing that will be the director's grand Donmar gesture of farewell. For quite a while, it looked as if Kidman would double as Yelena in *Uncle Vanya* and Olivia in *Twelfth Night* as part of an ensemble headed by Simon Russell Beale, the actor whom Mendes over the years has worked with most. (These plays mark their fifth and sixth collaborations, having already done four Shakespeares together.) Kidman says she "almost did do [the plays]," but the one-off opportunity of the Anthony Minghella film won out. "It was one of those things where I just went, 'I've got to do *Cold Mountain*.' And the thing that bums me is now I'll probably never get to be in *Vanya*."

Her loss soon became actress Helen McCrory's gain, with McCrory describing her reaction when she was told that she had got the roles first earmarked for Kidman. "It was the Nicole Kidman divorce day from Tom Cruise," laughs McCrory - "though Spitalfields isn't quite LA, you know". (The casting was especially sweet, since McCrory had been very much in the frame for *Proof*, pre-Paltrow.) The two shows' other primary female pairing is that of Sonya and Viola. And it was for that dual assignment that Mendes late in August, 2001, first met with Kate Winslet, a three-time Oscar nominee whose last theatre appearance had been a regional production of *What the Butler Saw* that happened well before *Titanic*. Winslet said no to the plays - "Kate wants to do theatre but short runs," explains Mendes (this commitment meant signing on for eight months, New York early in 2003 included) - but yes to the director, much to the excitement of a tabloid press in England that had been keen to marry off Mendes for years. (Winslet was considered early on for *Proof* but declined that, too.) Sonya and Viola, meanwhile, were passed to Emily Watson, herself no stranger to the Academy Awards, here returning to the London theatre for the first time since the 1994 National revival of Lillian Hellman's *The Children's Hour*.

McCrory and Watson are among the eleven performers gathered at the Vic this humid summer morning clutching scripts of *Twelfth Night*, the play that is to open second but begin rehearsals first.

Mendes is just back from a Chicago junket for *Road To Perdition*, having done one hundred thirty-four interviews on the trot: how many ways, he is wondering aloud, are there to explain what it was like working with Paul Newman?

Initial conversations are quick and often sweet. Simon Russell Beale, sporting stubble and a tan following a week's holiday in France, apologises to Emily Watson for not having seen *Gosford Park*. Paul Jesson, the Toby Belch in *Twelfth Night*, enthuses about a role that, he says, "I haven't played since I was sixteen." Helen McCrory admits to having phoned cast mate and friend Mark Strong over the weekend in a panic about which of the plays to prepare for today - a good thing, too, since she had embarked on the wrong one. Mendes has been in touch with Patsy Rodenburg about coming in for some voice work on the day the following week when he must be in New York for the gala premiere of *Road To Perdition*. (On that same day, the show's composer, George Stiles, will work with actor Anthony O'Donnell on the music for Feste.)

But the exigencies of Hollywood quickly evaporate once Mendes silences the group. "I'm extremely chuffed," he says, surveying the people around him, not least because, as he points out, "this is the last time I will be doing this" - as artistic director, that is, since Mendes talks of hoping to return to the Donmar as a guest, if his successor, Michael Grandage, will have him. One by one, Mendes works his way round the room, embracing some people, warmly characterising others: Newling gets introduced as "my co-dependent."

In some ways, this is to be an atypical readthrough. For one thing, Mendes himself will be reading - "butchering" is his word - the roles of Antonio and the Sea Captain, since cast member Gary Powell is away tending to an illness in the family. And though many rehearsal processes begin with statements of intention from the director, coupled with a tour of the set model from the designer, this one has neither. "I'm working in a much freer way than I ever have before," says Mendes. "I'm avoiding habits I have got used to in the past."

There will be ample opportunity ahead, one feels, for the director to communicate to the actors his affinities to these two plays. (Among them, Mendes on August 1, 2002, turned 37, the same age, he points out, as Astrov is in *Uncle Vanya*.) For now though, he tells me, "I'm intending to have a wonderful time; as my last show at the Donmar, that's my prerogative."

And within minutes, the company is seated round the oval table, scripts at the ready.

It's time to get to work.

Simon Russell Beale (top left then clockwise), Helen McCrory, Mark Strong and Emily Watson in *Uncle Vanya* ▶

chronology

1992-1993

Assassins
Comedy Shorts •
Richard III •
Playland
Don't Fool With Love •
Covent Garden Festival •
Translations
Here
The Life of Stuff
Hamlet •

1993-1994

Cabaret
Half Time •
Maria Friedman •
Beautiful Thing •
Helen Lederer •
Covent Garden Festival •
Glengarry Glen Ross
Design For Living
True West c

1994-1995

The Threepenny Opera
Highland Fling •
Our Boys c
Covent Garden Festival •
Insignificance
The Glass Menagerie
Rupert Street Lonely Hearts Club •

1995-1996

Company
The King of Prussia*
Buddleia*
Songs from a Forgotten City*
Bondagers*
Endgame
Habeas Corpus
Hedda Gabler •
Pentecost c
Fool for Love

1996-1997

Nine
Badfinger*
Summer Begins*
Halloween Night*
The Fix
The Maids
The Seagull •
Enter the Guardsman
Electra c

1997-1998

The Front Page
In a Little World of Our Own*
Tell Me*
Timeless*
Sleeping Around*
The Bullet
Three by Harold Pinter
How I Learned To Drive
Divas at the Donmar
The Blue Room

1998-1999

Into the Woods
Splash Hatch on the E Going Down*
Morphic Resonance*
Three Days of Rain*
Good
The Real Thing
Divas at the Donmar
Juno and the Paycock

1999-2000

Three Days of Rain
American Buffalo •
Helpless
Passion Play
Orpheus Descending
Divas at the Donmar
To the Green Fields Beyond

2000-2001

Merrily We Roll Along
Boston Marriage
Tales from Hollywood
A Lie of the Mind
Divas at the Donmar
The Little Foxes

2001-2002

Privates on Parade
Jesus Hopped the 'A' Train • c
Frame 312
Lobby Hero
Proof
Take Me Out c
Divas at the Donmar
Uncle Vanya
Twelfth Night

* - Carlton New Writing Season
c - Co-Production
• - Visiting Company

Assassins   22 October 1992 - 9 January 1993
British Premiere

Music and Lyrics:	Stephen Sondheim
Book:	John Weidman
Director:	Sam Mendes
Designer:	Anthony Ward
Lighting:	Paul Pyant
Musical Director:	Jeremy Sams
Sound:	John A Leonard
Cast:	Anthony Barclay, Paul Bentley, Cathryn Bradshaw, Michael Cantwell, Jack Ellis, Michelle Fine, David Firth, Louise Gold, Henry Goodman, Paul Harrhy, Ciaran Hinds, Sue Kelvin, Gareth Snook, Kevin Walton
Awards:	1992 Critics' Circle Award: Best New Musical
	1993 Laurence Oliver Award: Best Actor in a Musical (Henry Goodman)
	1993 Laurence Olivier Award nomination: Best Director of a Musical (Sam Mendes)
	1993 Laurence Olivier Award nomination: Best New Musical (Assassins)

Comedy Shorts   13 November 1992 - 2 January 1993
Late Night Comedy Performances

Jenny Éclair, Julie Balloo, Tom Hunsinger, Ben Keaton, Paul B Davies, Arthur Smith, Tony Hawks, Ben Miller, Robert Llewellyn, Maria McEarlane, Neil Mularkey, Louise Rennison

Richard III   14 January - 20 February 1993
RSC Tour

Writer:	William Shakespeare
Director:	Sam Mendes
Designer:	Tim Hatley
Lighting:	Paul Pyant
Composer:	Paddy Cunneen
Cast:	Annabelle Apsion, Simon Russell Beale, Mark Benton, Stephen Boxer, Simon Dormandy, Mike Dowling, Kate Duchene, Sam Graham, Ellie Haddington, Mark Lewis Jones, Cherry Morris, Michael Packer, Daniel Ryan, John Warnaby

Playland

British Premiere

Writer and Director: Athol Fugard
Designer: Susan Hilferty
Lighting: Mannie Manim
Sound: Mark Malherbe

Cast: John Kani, Sean Taylor

Don't Fool With Love

22 April - 15 May 1993

Cheek By Jowl

Writer: Alfred de Musset
Director: Declan Donnellan
Designer: Nick Ormerod
Composer: Paddy Cunneen
Movement Director: Jane Gibson
Lighting: Judith Greenwood

Cast: Patrick Bridgman, David Foxxe, Colin McFarlane, Maria Miles, Brian Pettifer, Pooky Quesnel, Michael Sheen, Anne White

Covent Garden Festival

18 - 31 May 1993

ENO Soundbites, Kit and the Widow, Music Box, Ian Stuart, Jill Gomez and John Constable, National Theatre Company, Brigit Nilsson, EOS, Chamber Made Opera, La Grande Scena, Opera Circus

Translations

3 June - 24 July 1993

Writer: Brian Friel
Director: Sam Mendes
Designer: Johan Engels
Lighting: Paul Pyant
Composer: Robert A White

Cast: Clare Cathcart, Daniel Flynn, Cara Kelly, David Killick, James Larkin, Barry Lynch, Robert Patterson, Norman Rodway, Tony Rohr, Zara Turner

1993

Here
9 July - 11 September 1993

World Premiere

Writer:	Michael Frayn
Director:	Michael Blakemore
Designer:	Ashley Martin-Davis
Lighting:	Mark Henderson
Cast:	Teresa Banham, Brenda Bruce, Iain Glen

The Life of Stuff
16 September - 6 November 1993

London Premiere

Writer:	Simon Donald
Director:	Matthew Warchus
Designer:	Neil Warmington
Lighting:	Rick Fisher
Sound:	Fergus O'Hare
Cast:	Mabel Aitken, Elizabeth Chadwick, Douglas Henshall, Sandy McDade, Stuart McQuarrie, Forbes Masson, Patrick O'Kane, Sean Scanlan
Awards:	1993 Evening Standard Award: Most Promising Playwright (Simon Donald)
	1993 Critics' Circle Award: Most Promising Playwright (Simon Donald)
	1994 Laurence Olivier Award nomination: Best Comedy (The Life of Stuff)
	1994 Laurence Olivier Award nomination: Best Actress in a Supporting Role (Sandy McDade)

Hamlet
10 - 27 November 1993

English Touring Theatre

Writer:	William Shakespeare
Director:	Stephen Unwin
Designer:	Bunnie Christie
Lighting:	Ben Ormerod
Composer:	Corin Buckeridge
Cast:	Mark Anstee, Andrew Ballington, James Barriscale, Trevor Baxter, Eleanor Bron, Alan Cumming, Pip Donaghy, Roger Hyams, David Joyce, William Key, Hilary Lyon, Ric Morgan, Alexander Nash

Cabaret   **2 December 1993 - 26 March 1994**

Book:	Joe Masteroff
Music:	John Kander
Lyrics:	Fred Ebb
Director:	Sam Mendes
Designer:	Sue Blane
Musical Director:	Paddy Cunneen
Choreographer:	Lea Anderson
Lighting:	Paul Pyant
Production	
Musical Director:	Jo Stewart
Sound:	John A Leonard

Cast: Alan Cumming, Michael Gardiner, Adam Godley, Jane Horrocks, Anthony Hunt, Matt Kane, Jane Karen, Sara Kestelman, Charlotte Medcalf, George Raistrick, Loveday Smith, Christopher Staines, Charlotte Storey, Kevin Walton

Awards: 1994 Laurence Olivier Award:
Best Supporting Performance in a Musical (Sara Kestelman)

1994 Laurence Olivier Award nomination:
Best Director of a Musical (Sam Mendes)

1994 Laurence Olivier Award nomination:
Best Actor in a Musical (Alan Cumming)

1994 Laurence Olivier Award nomination:
Best Musical Revival (Cabaret)

Televised by Carlton Television December 1994
A Roundabout Theatre production opened at the Henry Miller Theatre, New York
March - August 1998 and transferred to Studio 54 in September 1998

1998 Tony Award:
Best Actor in a Musical (Alan Cumming)

1998 Tony Award:
Best Actress in a Musical (Natasha Richardson)

1998 Tony Award:
Best Actor in a Musical - Featured Role (Ron Rifkin)

1998 Tony Award:
Best Musical Revival (Cabaret)

1998 Tony Award nomination:
Best Director of a Musical (Sam Mendes with Rob Marshall)

1998 Tony Award nomination:
Best Actress in a Musical - Featured Role (Mary Louise Wilson)

Cabaret awards continued

1998 Tony Award nomination:
Best Orchestrations (Michael Gibson)

1998 Tony Award nomination:
Best Costume Designer (William Ivey Long)

1998 Tony Award nomination:
Best Lighting Designer (Peggy Eisenhauer and Mike Baldassari)

1998 Tony Award nomination:
Best Choreographer (Rob Marshall)

3 Drama Desk Awards

3 Outer Critics' Circle Awards

Theatre World Award

Fred Astaire Award

New York Drama Critics' Award

Gold Camera Award for Televised Recording

Half Time   4, 5, 11 and 12 February 1994

Writers:	Richard Bonneville, Christopher Luscombe
Lighting:	Jonathan Richardson and Stuart Crane
Sound:	Fergus O'Hare
Cast:	Chris Luscombe

Maria Friedman by Special Arrangement
20, 27 February and 6 March 1994

Director:	Matthew White
Producer:	Sonia Friedman
Musical Director:	Michael Haslam
Lighting:	Stuart Crane
Sound:	Fergus O'Hare
Awards:	1995 Laurence Olivier Award:
	Best Entertainment (Maria Friedman)

Beautiful Thing
29 March - 23 April 1994

Bush Theatre

Writer:	Jonathan Harvey
Director:	Hettie McDonald
Designer:	Robin Don
Lighting:	Johanna Town
Sound:	Paul Bull
Cast:	Richard Bonneville, Amelda Brown, Shaun Digwall, Mark Letheren, Sophie Stanton
Awards:	1995 Laurence Olivier Award nomination: Best Comedy (Beautiful Thing)

Helen Lederer Still Crazy After All These Years 25 - 30 April 1994

Covent Garden Festival
9 - 21 May 1994

included La Traviata, The Wasteland and The Impro Musical

Awards:	1995 Laurence Olivier Award nomination: Outstanding Achievement in Opera (La Traviata)

Maria Friedman
by Special Arrangement by Further Arrangement
23 May - 11 June 1994

Director:	Jeremy Sams
Designer:	Lez Brotherson
Musical Director:	Michael Haslam
Lighting:	Jonathan Richardson
Sound:	John A Leonard

Transferred to the Whitehall Theatre as "Maria Friedman by Extra Special Arrangement"
May - June 1995

Glengarry Glen Ross
16 June - 27 August 1994

Writer:	David Mamet
Director:	Sam Mendes
Designer:	Johan Engels
Lighting:	David Hersey
Sound:	Fergus O'Hare
Cast:	William Armstrong, Keith Bartlett, John Benfield, James Bolam, Ron Cook, Tony O'Donnell, Carl Proctor

Glengarry Glen Ross continued

Awards:　1995 Laurence Olivier Award nomination:
Best Actor (James Bolam)

1995 Laurence Olivier Award nomination:
Best Lighting Designer (David Hersey)

Design for Living　　1 September - 5 November 1994

Writer:　Noël Coward
Director:　Sean Mathias
Designer:　Stephen Brimson Lewis
Lighting:　Mark Henderson
Composer:　Jason Carr
Sound:　John A Leonard

Cast:　Stuart Bennett, Jason Cheater, Nicholas Clay, Jan de Villeneuve, Lou Gish, Johanna Kirby, Clive Owen, Paul Rhys, Chad Shepherd, Rachel Weisz

Awards:　1994 Evening Standard Award:
Best Director (Sean Mathias)

1994 Evening Standard Award:
Best Lighting Designer (Mark Henderson)

1994 Critics' Circle Award:
Best Director (Sean Mathias)

1994 Critics' Circle Award:
Most Promising Newcomer (Rachel Weisz)

1995 Laurence Olivier Award:
Best Set Designer (Stephen Brimson Lewis)

1995 Laurence Olivier Award nomination:
Best Costume Designer (Stephen Brimson Lewis)

Transferred to the Gielgud Theatre February - June 1995. Presented by Bill Kenwright Ltd

True West　　9 November - 3 December 1994

A co-production with West Yorkshire Playhouse

Writer:　Sam Shepard
Director:　Matthew Warchus
Designer:　Rob Howell
Lighting:　Alan Burrett
Composer:　Claire Van Kampen

Cast:　David Henry, Michael Rudko, Mark Rylance, Marcia Warren

True West *continued*

Transferred to the Circle in the Square Theatre, New York March - July 2000

Awards:
    2000 Tony Award nomination:
    Best Actor (Philip Seymour Hoffman)

    2000 Tony Award nomination:
    Best Actor (John C Reilly)

    2000 Tony Award nomination:
    Best Play (True West)

    2000 Tony Award nomination:
    Best Director (Matthew Warchus)

    2000 Special Achievement Award:
    Philip Seymour Hoffman and John C Reilly

The Threepenny Opera   **8 December 1994 -18 March 1995**

Book and Lyrics:	Bertolt Brecht
Music:	Kurt Weill
Translation:	Robert David McDonald
New Lyric Translation:	Jeremy Sams
Director:	Phyllida Lloyd
Designer:	Vicki Mortimer
Musical Director:	Gary Yershon
Lighting:	Rick Fisher
Sound:	Paul Arditti
Choreographer:	Quinny Sacks
Production Musical Director:	Kate Edgar
Cast:	Ben Albu, Natasha Bain, Simon Dormandy, Jeremy Harrison, Tom Hollander, Tara Hugo, Beverly Klein, Tom Mannion, Terence Maynard, Dawn Michaels, Sharon Small, Simon Walter

Awards:
    1995 Laurence Olivier Award nomination:
    Best Supporting Performance in a Musical (Tara Hugo)

    1995 Laurence Olivier award nomination:
    Best Musical Revival (The Threepenny Opera)

Cast Recording by That's Entertainment

Highland Fling

21 March - 8 April 1995

Adventures in Motion Pictures

Director and Choreographer:	Matthew Bourne
Composer:	Herman Severin Lovenskiold
Designer:	Lez Brotherson
Company:	Rosemary Allen, Scott Ambler, Maxine Fone, Andrew George, Phil Hill, Isabel Mortimer, Emily Pierce

Our Boys

11 April - 13 May 1995

A Derby Playhouse co-production with Rupert Gavin for Incidental Theatre

Writer and Director:	Jonathan Lewis
Designer:	Niki Turner
Lighting:	Tim Mitchell
Composer:	Colin Good
Cast:	Marston Bloom, Ian Dunn, Perry Fenwick (to 22 April), Sean Gilder, Lloyd Owen, Steve Sweeney (from 24 April), Jake Wood

Covent Garden Festival

15 - 27 May 1995

included The Magic Flute

Insignificance

1 June - 6 August 1995

Writer and Director:	Terry Johnson
Designer:	Mark Thompson
Lighting:	Hugh Vanstone
Sound:	John A Leonard
Cast:	Alun Armstrong, Frances Barber, Ian Hogg, Jack Klaff

The Glass Menagerie

7 September - 5 November 1995

Writer:	Tennessee Williams
Director:	Sam Mendes
Designer:	Rob Howell
Lighting:	David Hersey
Music:	Jason Carr
Sound:	Scott Myers
Cast:	Ben Chaplin, Mark Dexter, Claire Skinner, Zoë Wanamaker

The Glass Menagerie continued

Awards: 1995 Critics' Circle Award:
Best Director (Sam Mendes)

1995 Critics' Circle Award:
Best Actress (Claire Skinner)

1995 Time Out Award:
Best Performance Off-West End (Claire Skinner)

1996 Laurence Olivier Award:
Best Director (Sam Mendes)

1996 Laurence Olivier Award:
Best Lighting (David Hersey)

1996 Laurence Olivier Award nomination:
Best Actress (Zoë Wanamaker)

1996 Laurence Olivier Award nomination:
Best Set Designer (Rob Howell)

1996 Laurence Olivier Award nomination:
Best Supporting Performance (Claire Skinner)

1996 Laurence Olivier Award nomination:
Best Supporting Performance (Ben Chaplin)

Transferred to the Comedy Theatre December 1995 - March 1996. Presented by Thelma Holt Ltd

Rupert Street Lonely Hearts Club   7- 25 November 1995

English Touring Theatre and Contact Theatre Company

Writer:	Jonathan Harvey
Director:	John Burgess
Designer:	Jackie Brooks
Lighting:	Gerry Jenkinson
Cast:	Elizabeth Berrington, James Bowers, Lorraine Brunning, Tom Higgins, Scot Williams

1995/6 DONMAR

Company 1 December 1995 - 2 March 1996

Music and Lyrics:	Stephen Sondheim
Book:	George Furth
Director:	Sam Mendes
Designer:	Mark Thompson
Production Musical Director:	Gareth Valentine
Orchestrations:	Jonathan Tunick
Lighting:	Paul Pyant
Musical Staging:	Jonathan Butterell
Musical Director:	Paddy Cunneen
Sound:	John A Leonard
Cast:	Paul Bentley, Clare Burt, Anna Francolini, Rebecca Front, Sheila Gish, Kiran Hocking, Hannah James, Teddy Kempner, Adrian Lester, Clive Rowe, Liza Sadovy, Michael Simkins, Gareth Snook, Sophie Thompson

Awards:

1995 Critics' Circle Award:
Best Musical (Company)
1995 Critics' Circle Award:
Best Director (Sam Mendes)
1996 Laurence Olivier Award:
Best Director (Sam Mendes)

1996 Laurence Olivier Award:
Best Actor in a Musical (Adrian Lester)

1996 Laurence Olivier Award:
Best Supporting Performance in a Musical (Sheila Gish)

1996 Laurence Olivier Award nomination:
Best Supporting Performance in a Musical (Sophie Thomson)

1996 Music Industry Award for cast recording

Transferred to the Albery Theatre March - June 1996. Presented by Bill Kenwright Ltd.

Televised for BBC2 Performance Series, broadcast March 1997

Cast Recording by First Night Records

---

4 Corners Carlton Season of New Writing 4 March - 6 April 1996
The King of Prussia 4 - 9 March

Kneehigh Theatre Company

Writer:	Nick Darke
Director:	Mike Shepherd
Designer:	Bill Mitchell
Lighting:	Alan Drake
Musical Director:	Jim Carey

The King of Prussia continued

Cast:	Bec Applebee, Charlie Barnecut, Carl Grose, Giles King, Tristan Sturrock, Mary Woodvine

Buddleia   12 - 16 March
The Passion Machine

Writer and Director:	Paul Mercier
Design:	Anne Gately
Lighting:	Megan Sheppard
Music:	John Dunne
Cast:	Alan Archbold, Charlotte Bradley, Des Braiden, Liam Carney, Denis Conway, Donagh Deeney, Stephen Dunne, Robert English, Berts Folan, David Gorry, Michelle Houlden, Eamonn Hunt, Alan King, Brendan Laird, Jack Lynch, Eanna MacLiam, Brid McCarthy, Pat McGrath, Bernadette McKenna, Johnny Murphy, Ruth Murphy, Mick Nolan, Enda Oates, Frank O'Sullivan, Caroline Rothwell, Karen Scully, Birdy Sweeney, Tony Tormey, Catherine Walsh, Barry Ward

Songs from a Forgotten City   18 - 23 March
Y Cymni

Writer and Director:	Edward Thomas
Design:	Jane Linz Roberts
Lighting:	Nick MacLiammoir
Composer:	John Hardy
Sound Design:	Mike Beer
Cast:	Patrick Brennan, Russell Gomer, Jack James

Bondagers   27 March - 6 April
The Traverse Theatre

Writer:	Sue Glover
Director:	Ian Brown
Designer:	Stewart Laing
Lighting:	Paule Constable
Composer:	Pete Livingstone
Cast:	Carol Ann Crawford, Julie Duncanson, Kathryn Howden, Hilary MacLean, Rosaleen Pelan, Ann-Louise Ross

1996

Endgame

11 April - 25 May 1996

Writer:	Samuel Beckett
Director:	Katie Mitchell
Designer:	Rae Smith
Costume:	Johanna Coe
Movement:	Struan Leslie
Lighting:	Chris Davey
Sound:	Fergus O'Hare
Cast:	Alun Armstrong, Stephen Dillane, Harry Jones, Eileen Nicholas
Awards:	1996 Time Out Award: Best Director Off-West End (Katie Mitchell)

Habeas Corpus

30 May - 27 July 1996

Writer:	Alan Bennett
Director:	Sam Mendes
Designer:	Rob Howell
Lighting:	Paul Pyant
Music:	George Stiles
Movement:	Jonathan Butterell
Sound:	Fergus O'Hare
Performance Musical Director:	Michael Haslam
Costume Supervisor:	Lynette Mauro
Cast:	Brenda Blethyn, Hugh Bonneville, Jim Broadbent, Celia Imrie, John Padden, Stewart Permutt, Imelda Staunton, Natalie Walter, Jason Watkins, Nicholas Woodeson, Sarah Woodward

Hedda Gabler

30 July - 31 August 1996

English Touring Theatre

Writer:	Henrik Ibsen
Director:	Stephen Unwin
Designer:	Pamela Howard
Lighting:	Ben Ormerod
Music:	Corin Buckeridge
Cast:	Mary Chester, Ann Firbank, Alexander Gilbreath, David Killick, Crispin Letts, Jonathan Phillips, Carol Starks

Pentecost

3 - 28 September 1996

A co-production with Rough Magic Theatre Company

Writer:	Stewart Parker
Director:	Lynne Parker
Designer:	Blaithin Sheerin
Lighting:	Stephen McManus
Cast:	Brian Doherty, Michele Forbes, Paul Hickey, Eleanor Methven, Morna Regan

Fool for Love

3 October - 30 November 1996

Writer:	Sam Shepard
Director:	Ian Brown
Set Designer:	Robin Don
Costume Designer:	Tanya McCallin
Music:	Phillip Dupuy
Lighting:	Howard Harrison
Sound:	John A Leonard
Cast:	Lorraine Ashbourne, Gawn Grainger, Barry Lynch, Martin Marquez

Nine

6 December 1996 - 8 March 1997

Music and Lyrics:	Maury Yeston
Book:	Arthur Kopit
Director:	David Leveaux
Designer:	Anthony Ward
Musical Director:	Gareth Valentine
Lighting:	Paul Pyant
Choreographer:	Jonathan Butterell
Orchestration:	Mark Warman
Assistant MD:	Matthew Freeman
Sound:	John A Leonard and John Owens
Cast:	Norma Atallah, Clare Burt, Ian Covington, Eleanor David, Emma Dears, Susie Dumbreck, Susannah Fellows, Jenny Galloway, Kiran Hocking, Owen Proctor Jackson, Ria Jones, Sara Kestelman, Larry Lamb, Dilys Laye, Kristin Marks, Stuart Neal, Sarah Parish, Tessa Pritchard, Norma West
Awards:	1997 Laurence Olivier Award nomination: Best New Musical (Nine) Best Musical (Nine)

4 Corners Carlton Season of New Writing 11 March - 19 April 1997

Badfinger   11 - 22 March

Thin Language Theatre Company

Writer:	Simon Harris
Director:	Michael Sheen
Designer:	Andrew Harrison
Lighting:	David Plater
Cast:	Robert Blythe, Rhodri Hugh, Jason Hughes, Rhys Ifans, Richard Mylan

Summer Begins   25 March - 5 April

In association with the National Theatre Studio

Writer:	David Eldridge
Director:	Jonathan Lloyd
Designer:	Conor Murphy
Lighting:	David Plater
Sound:	Sebastian Frost
Cast:	Elizabeth Chadwick, Beatie Edney, Darren Tighe, Heather Tobias, Gary Webster

Halloween Night   8 - 19 April

Rough Magic Theatre Company

Writer:	Declan Hughes
Director:	Lynne Parker
Designer:	Kathy Strachan
Lighting:	Stephen McManus
Cast:	Pom Boyd, Anne Byrne, Miche Doherty, Paul Hickey, Jenni Ledwell, Eanna MacLiam, Michael McElhatton, Sean Rocks, Simon O'Gorman, Arthur Riordan

The Fix
26 April - 14 June 1997
World Premiere
Produced in association with Cameron Mackintosh

Book and Lyrics:	John Dempsey
Music:	Dana P. Rowe
Director:	Sam Mendes
Choreography:	Charles Augins
Designer:	Rob Howell
Lighting:	Howard Harrison
Sound:	Andrew Bruce and Bobby Aitken
Orchestrations:	Steve Margoshes
Musical Supervisor:	David Caddick
Musical Director:	Colin Welford
Cast:	David Bardsley, John Barrowman, Krysten Cummings, Carrie Ellis, Kathryn Evans, David Firth, Mark Frendo, Christina Fry, Thomas Hawes, Christopher Holt, Gael Johnson, Bogdan Kominowski, Thomas Moll, John Partridge, Nicholas Pound, Archie Preston, Philip Quast, Richard D Sharp, Hannah Tollman
Awards:	1998 Laurence Olivier Award: Best Actor in a Musical (Philip Quast)
	1998 Laurence Olivier Award nomination: Best Lighting Designer (Howard Harrison)
	1998 Laurence Olivier Award nomination: Best Actor in a Musical (John Barrowman)
	1998 Laurence Olivier Award nomination: Best New Musical (The Fix)

The Maids
19 June - 9 August 1997

Writer:	Jean Genet
Translation:	David Rudkin
Director:	John Crowley
Designer:	Tim Hatley
Music:	Paddy Cunneen
Movement:	Jonathan Butterell
Lighting:	Rick Fisher
Sound:	John A Leonard
Cast:	Niamh Cusack, Kerry Fox, Josette Simon

The Maids toured to the Yvonne Arnaud Theatre, Guildford; Theatre Royal, Bath; Liverpool Everyman and Richmond Theatre. Presented by Thelma Holt Ltd

The Seagull
12 August - 6 September 1997

English Touring Theatre

Writer:	Anton Chekhov
Director:	Stephen Unwin
Scenographer:	Pamela Howard
Lighting:	Ben Ormerod
Music:	Corin Buckeridge
Sound:	Frank Bradley
Cast:	Mark Bazeley, Duncan Bell, Cheryl Campbell, Abigail Duddleston, Sandra Duncan, Christopher Good, Colin Haigh, Denys Hawthorne, Sarah-Jane Holm, Alan Leith, Joanna Roth, Paul Slack

Enter the Guardsman
11 September - 18 October 1997

Based on the Guardsman by Ferenc Molnár

World Premiere

Book:	Scott Wentworth
Music:	Craig Bohmler
Lyrics:	Marion Adler
Director:	Jeremy Sams
Designer:	Francis O'Connor
Musical Director:	Mark Warman
Orchestrations:	David Firman
Lighting:	Mark Henderson
Sound:	John A Leonard
Musical Staging:	Andrew George
Cast:	Janie Dee, Walter Van Dyk, Jeremy Finch, Alexander Hanson, Nicky Henson, Angela Richards, Nicola Sloane
Awards:	1998 Laurence Olivier Award nomination: Best Supporting Performance in a Musical (Nicky Henson)
	1998 Laurence Olivier Award nomination: Best New Musical (Enter The Guardsman)

Electra

21 October - 6 December 1997

A co-production with Chichester Festival Theatre

Writer:	Sophocles
New Version:	Frank McGuinness
Director:	David Leveaux
Designer:	Johan Engels
Lighting:	Paul Pyant
Movement:	Jonathan Butterell
Sound:	Fergus O'Hare
Cast:	Roger Braban, Orla Charlton, Jenny Galloway, Andrew Howard, Alison Johnston, Martin McKellan, Raad Rawi, Ninka Scott, Rudolph Walker, Zoë Wanamaker, Marjorie Yates
Awards:	1998 Variety Club Award:
	Best Actress (Zoë Wanamaker)
	1998 Laurence Olivier Award:
	Best Actress (Zoë Wanamaker)

Transferred to the McCarter Theatre, Princeton, New Jersey September - October 1998 and the Barrymore Theatre, New York November 1998 - March 1999

> 1999 Tony Award nomination:
> Best Actress (Zoë Wanamaker)
>
> 1999 Tony Award nomination:
> Best Actress - Featured Role (Clare Bloom)
>
> 1999 Tony Award nomination:
> Best Play Revival (Electra)

The Front Page

10 December 1997 - 28 February 1998

Writers:	Ben Hecht and Charles MacArthur
Director:	Sam Mendes
Designer:	Mark Thompson
Lighting:	Hugh Vanstone
Sound:	John A Leonard and John Owens
Costume:	Irene Bohan
Dialect Coach:	Joan Washington
Cast:	Alun Armstrong, Ian Bartholomew, Keith Bartlett, Christopher Benjamin, Mark Benton, Neil Caple, Ian Gelder, Nicholas Gleaves, Adam Godley, Simon Gregor, John Hodgkinson, Rebecca Johnson, Martin Marquez, Lizzy McInnerny, Tim McMullan, Hilton McRae, Sara Pelosi, Griff Rhys Jones, Tilly Tremayne

1998

4 Corners Carlton Season of New Writing

In a Little World of our Own

3 - 28 March 1998

3 - 7 March

The Foundry

Writer:	Gary Mitchell
Director:	Robert Delamere
Designer:	Simon Higlett
Lighting:	Chris Davey
Composer:	Dominic Shovelton
Cast:	Lorcan Cranitch, Colin Farrell, Stuart Graham, Paul Hickey, Helen McCrory

Tell Me

9 - 14 March

Northern Stage

Writer:	Matthew Dunster
Director:	Richard Gregory
Designer:	Simon Banham
Lighting:	Mike Brookes
Sound and Composer:	John Kefala Kerr
Choreography:	Jane Mason
Cast:	Ben Crompton, Ben Joiner, David Whitaker, Gillian Wright

Timeless

17 - 21 March

Suspect Culture

Writer:	David Greig
Director:	Graham Eatough
Designer:	Ian Scott
Music:	Nick Powell
Cast:	Kate Dickie, Paul Thomas Hickey, Molly Innes, Keith Macpherson

Sleeping Around

23 - 28 March

Paines Plough

Writers:	Hilary Fanin, Stephen Greenhorn, Abi Morgan and Mark Ravenhill
Director:	Vicky Featherstone
Designer:	Georgia Sion
Cast:	John Lloyd Fillingham, Sophie Stanton

The Bullet
World Premiere   **2 April - 2 May 1998**

Writer:	Joe Penhall
Director:	Dominic Cooke
Designer:	Christopher Oram
Lighting:	Howard Harrison
Sound:	Fergus O'Hare
Cast:	Miles Anderson, Barbara Flynn, Neil Stuke, Andrew Tiernan, Emily Woof

Three by Harold Pinter   **7 May - 13 June 1998**

A Kind of Alaska

Writer:	Harold Pinter
Director:	Karel Reisz
Designer:	Tom Rand
Lighting:	Robert Bryan
Sound:	John A Leonard
Cast:	Brid Brennan, Bill Nighy, Penelope Wilton

The Lover and The Collection

Writer:	Harold Pinter
Director:	Joe Harmston
Designer:	Tom Rand
Lighting:	Robert Bryan
Sound:	John A Leonard
Cast:	Douglas Hodge, Colin McFarlane, Harold Pinter, Lia Williams

The Lover and The Collection toured to the Theatre Royal, Bath and Richmond Theatre

How I Learned To Drive
British Premiere   **18 June - 8 August 1998**

Writer:	Paula Vogel
Director:	John Crowley
Designer:	Rob Howell
Lighting:	Paul Pyant
Movement:	Jonathan Butterell
Sound:	Fergus O'Hare
Cast:	Michael Colgan, Jenny Galloway, Helen McCrory, Phillippa Stanton, Kevin Whately

Divas at the Donmar
10 August - 5 September 1998

Designer:	Robert Jones
Lighting:	Howard Harrison and Stuart Crane
Sound:	Andy Brown

Ann Hampton Callaway and Liz Callaway - Sibling Revelry

Director:	Dan Foster
Musical Director:	Alex Rybeck

Barbara Cook

Musical Director:	Willy Harper

Imelda Staunton and Her Big Band

Musical Director:	Nick Lloyd

The Blue Room
17 September - 31 October 1998

Freely adapted from Arthur Schnitzler's La Ronde

World Premiere

Writer:	David Hare
Director:	Sam Mendes
Designer:	Mark Thompson
Lighting:	Hugh Vanstone
Music:	Paddy Cunneen
Sound:	Scott Myers
Cast:	Iain Glen, Nicole Kidman
Awards:	1998 Evening Standard Award:
	Outstanding Contribution to London Theatre (Nicole Kidman)
	1999 Laurence Olivier Award:
	Best Lighting (Hugh Vanstone)
	1999 Laurence Olivier Award nomination:
	Best Actress (Nicole Kidman)
	1999 Laurence Olivier Award nomination:
	Best Actor (Iain Glen)
	1999 Laurence Olivier Award nomination:
	Best Director (Sam Mendes)
	1999 Laurence Olivier Award nomination:
	Best Set Design (Mark Thompson)
	1999 Laurence Olivier Award nomination:
	Best Play of the Year (David Hare)

Transferred to the Cort Theatre, New York December 1998 - February 1999

Into the Woods   6 November 1998 - 13 February 1999

Music and Lyrics:	Stephen Sondheim
Book:	James Lapine
Director:	John Crowley
Co-Director and Choreographer:	Jonathan Butterell
Designer:	Bob Crowley
Lighting:	Paul Pyant
Original Orchestrations:	Jonathan Tunick
Musical Director and Orchestrations:	Mark Warman
Sound:	John A Leonard
Cast:	Michelle Blair, Clare Burt, Louise Davidson, Ceri Anne Gregory, Michael N. Harbour, Nick Holder, Samantha Lavender, Dilys Laye, Damian Lewis, Frank Middlemass, Christopher Pizzey, Matt Rawle, Sheila Reid, Jenna Russell, Caroline Sheen, Sheridan Smith, Sophie Thompson, Tony Timberlake, Zoë Walsham
Awards:	1999 Laurence Olivier Award: Best Actress in a Musical (Sophie Thompson) 1999 Laurence Olivier Award nomination: Outstanding Musical Production (Into the Woods)

American Imports:
The Carlton Season of New Writing   16 February - 13 March 1999

Designer:	Tom Piper
Lighting:	David Plater
Sound:	Rob Tory

Splash Hatch on the E Going Down   16 - 27 February

Writer:	Kia Corthron
Director:	Roxana Silbert
Cast:	Brian Bovell, Chiwetel Ejiofor, Tameka Empson, Shauna Shim, Naomi Wirthner

Morphic Resonance   17 - 27 February

Writer:	Katherine Burger
Director:	James Kerr
Cast:	Michael Culkin, Anastasia Hille, Nigel Lindsay, Lloyd Owen, Joanna Roth

American Imports: The Carlton Season of New Writing continued

Three Days of Rain
1 - 13 March

Writer: Richard Greenberg
Director: Robin Lefevre
Cast: Colin Firth, Elizabeth McGovern, David Morrissey

Awards: 1999 Evening Standard Award nomination:
Best Actor (Colin Firth)

Good
18 March - 22 May 1999

Writer: CP Taylor
Director: Michael Grandage
Designer: Christopher Oram
Lighting: Hartley T A Kemp
Musical Supervisor: Michael Haslam
Sound: John A Leonard
Cast: Cymon Allen, Faith Brook, Eva Marie Bryer, Charles Dance, Emilia Fox, Ian Gelder, Peter Moreton, John Ramm, Benedict Taylor, Jessica Turner

Awards: 1999 Evening Standard Award nomination:
Best Actor (Charles Dance)

The Real Thing
27 May - 7 August 1999

Writer: Tom Stoppard
Director: David Leveaux
Designer: Vicki Mortimer
Lighting: Mark Henderson
Sound: John A Leonard
Cast: Mark Bazeley, Stephen Dillane, Jennifer Ehle, Caroline Hayes, Joshua Henderson, Nigel Lindsay, Sarah Woodward

Awards: 1999 Evening Standard Award:
Best Actor (Stephen Dillane)

2000 Laurence Olivier Award:
Best Lighting Designer (Mark Henderson)

2000 Laurence Olivier Award nomination:
Best Actress (Jennifer Ehle)

2000 Laurence Olivier Award nomination:
Best Actor (Stephen Dillane)

2000 Laurence Olivier Award nomination:
Best Director (David Leveaux)

The Real Thing continued

Transferred to the Albery Theatre January - March 2000

Cast: Stephen Dillane, Alex Dunbar, Jennifer Ehle, Tabitha Fielding,
Joshua Henderson, Nigel Lindsay, Guy Manning, Charlotte Parry,
Oscar Pearce, Victoria Pritchard, Sarah Woodward

Transferred to the Barrymore Theatre, New York March - August 2000

2000 Tony Award:

Best Actor (Stephen Dillane)

2000 Tony Award:

Best Actress (Jennifer Ehle)

2000 Tony Award:

Best Play Revival (The Real Thing)

2000 Tony Award nomination:

Best Actress - Featured Role (Sara Woodward)

2000 Tony Award nomination: Best Director (David Leveaux)

2 Drama Desk Awards

Drama League Award

Divas at the Donmar   9 August - 4 September 1999

Designer: Robert Jones

Lighting Design: Howard Harrison and Stuart Crane

Sound Design: Andy Brown in association with Mark Fiore

Patti LuPone - Matters of the Heart

Director: Scott Wittman

Musical Director
and Arranger: Dick Gallagher

Make up and Hair: Danielle Vignjevich

Audra McDonald - Way Back to Paradise

Musical Director: Ted Sperling

Sam Brown with Mystic Oyster

1999/2000   **DONMAR**

Juno and the Paycock   **9 September - 6 November 1999**

Writer: Sean O'Casey
Director: John Crowley
Designer: Rae Smith
Lighting: Hugh Vanstone
Sound: Fergus O'Hare
Cast: Tom Ambrose, William Ash, Jonathan Bond, David Carey, Ron Cook,
                 Stephen Kennedy, Colm Meaney, Dearbhla Molloy, Damian O'Hare
                 Helen Ryan, Bernadette Shortt, Renee Weldon

Awards: 2000 Laurence Olivier Award nomination:
                 Best Supporting Actor (Ron Cook)

Transferred to the Gramercy Theatre, New York September - December 2000

Three Days of Rain   **9 November - 22 December 1999**
                                         and 5 - 22 January 2000

Writer: Richard Greenberg
Director: Robin Lefevre
Designer: Tom Piper
Lighting: Dave Plater
Costumes: Lorna Marshall
Music: Phillip Dupuy
Sound: Rob Tory
Cast: Colin Firth, Elizabeth McGovern, David Morrissey

Awards: 1999 Evening Standard Award nomination:
                 Best Actor (Colin Firth)

                 2000 Laurence Olivier Award nomination:
                 Play of the Year (Three Days Of Rain)

American Buffalo   **28 January - 26 February 2000**

A co-production with the Atlantic Theater Company

Writer: David Mamet
Director: Neil Pepe
Set Designer: Kevin Rigdon
Lighting: Howard Werner
Sound: Rob Tory
Costumes: Laura Bauer
Cast: Philip Baker Hall, William H Macy, Mark Webber

Transferred to the Atlantic Theater, New York March - May 2000

Helpless   2 March - 8 April 2000

Writer:	Dusty Hughes
Director:	Robin Lefevre
Designer:	Tom Piper
Lighting:	Mick Hughes
Sound:	John A. Leonard
Cast:	Ron Cook, Charlotte Cornwell, Julie Graham, Craig Kelly, Art Malik, Rachael Stirling

Passion Play   13 April - 10 June 2000

Writer:	Peter Nichols
Director:	Michael Grandage
Designer:	Christopher Oram
Lighting:	Hartley T A Kemp
Sound:	Fergus O'Hare
Cast:	Gillian Barge, Ruth Brennan, Cheryl Campbell, Martin Jarvis, Toni Kanal, Arthur Kelly, James Laurenson, Cherie Lunghi, Francis Maguire, Nicola Walker, Peter Winnall
Awards:	2000 Evening Standard Award: Best Director (Michael Grandage)
	2001 Critics' Circle Award: Best Director (Michael Grandage)
	2001 Laurence Olivier Award nomination: Best Director (Michael Grandage)
	2001 Laurence Olivier Award nomination: Best Supporting Actress (Gillian Barge)

Transferred to the Comedy Theatre June - August 2000

Cast:	Gillian Barge, Cheryl Campbell, Heather Craney, Nicky Henson, Judith Hepburn, Toni Kanal, Arthur Kelly, James Laurenson, Cherie Lunghi, Tom Marshall, Francis Maguire, Katherine Stark, Nicola Walker, Peter Winnall

Orpheus Descending

15 June - 12 August 2000

Writer:	Tennessee Williams
Director:	Nicholas Hytner
Designer:	Bob Crowley
Lighting:	Hugh Vanstone
Music:	Keith Williams
Sound:	John A Leonard and Fergus O'Hare
Cast:	Ilario Bisi-Pedro, Sandra Dickinson, Richard Durden, Janet Henfrey, William Hootkins, Tom Hunsinger, Kristin Marks, Helen Mirren, Martin Potter, Saskia Reeves, Anne Ridler, Jason Salkey, Lolly Susi, Julia Swift, Stuart Townsend

Awards   2001 Laurence Olivier Award nomination: Best Actress (Helen Mirren)

Divas at the Donmar

21 August - 9 September 2000

Designer:	Robert Jones
Lighting:	Howard Harrison and Stuart Crane
Sound:	Andy Brown

Betty Buckley

Musical Director:	Kenny Werner

Clive Rowe

Musical Director:	Wendy Gadian
Musical Arrangements:	Neil McArthur

To the Green Fields Beyond

14 September - 25 November 2000

World Premiere

Writer:	Nick Whitby
Director:	Sam Mendes
Designer:	Anthony Ward
Lighting:	Howard Harrison
Music:	Stephen Warbeck
Sound:	John A Leonard
Cast:	Danny Babington, Hugh Dancy, Nitin Ganatra, Johanna Lonsky, Finbar Lynch, Gary Powell, Danny Sapani, Adrian Scarborough, Dougray Scott, Paul Venables, Ray Winstone

Awards: 2001 Laurence Olivier Award nomination: Best Lighting Designer (Howard Harrison)

Merrily We Roll Along   **1 December 2000 - 3 March 2001**

Music and Lyrics:	Stephen Sondheim
Book:	George Furth
Director:	Michael Grandage
Designer:	Christopher Oram
Lighting:	Tim Mitchell
Musical Director:	Gareth Valentine
New Orchestrations:	Jonathan Tunick
Choreography:	Peter Darling
Sound:	Fergus O'Hare
Cast:	Matt Blair, Lucy Bradshaw, Daniel Evans, Anna Francolini, Neil Gordon-Taylor, Dean Hussain, David Lucas, James Millard, Zehra Neqvi, Julian Ovenden, Grant Russell, Samantha Spiro, Mary Stockley, Emma Jay Thomas, Shona White
Awards:	2000 Critics' Circle Award: Best Director (Michael Grandage)
	2001 Laurence Olivier Award: Best Actor in a Musical (Daniel Evans)
	2001 Laurence Olivier Award: Best Actress in a Musical (Samantha Spiro)
	2001 Laurence Olivier Award: Best New Musical (Merrily We Roll Along)
	2001 Laurence Olivier Award nomination: Best Theatre Choreographer (Peter Darling)
	2001 Evening Standard Award nomination: Best Musical (Merrily We Roll Along)

Boston Marriage   **8 March - 14 April 2001**
European Premiere

Writer:	David Mamet
Director:	Phyllida Lloyd
Designer:	Peter McKintosh
Lighting:	Rick Fisher
Music:	Gary Yershon
Cast:	Anna Chancellor, Lyndsey Marshal, Zoë Wanamaker
Awards:	2001 Critics' Circle Award: Most Promising Newcomer (Lyndsey Marshal)
	2002 Laurence Olivier Award nomination: Best Actress (Zoë Wanamaker)

2001

Boston Marriage awards continued

2002 Laurence Olivier Award nomination:
Best Actress in a Supporting Role (Lyndsey Marshal)

2002 Laurence Olivier Award nomination:
Best New Comedy (Boston Marriage)

2001 Evening Standard Award nomination:
Outstanding Newcomer (Lyndsey Marshal)

Transferred to the New Ambassadors Theatre November 2001 - February 2002

Tales from Hollywood   19 April - 23 June 2001

Writer:	Christopher Hampton
Director:	John Crowley
Designer:	Scott Pask
Lighting:	Howard Harrison
Associate Costume Designer:	Irene Bohan
Music:	Paddy Cunneen
Sound:	Paul Arditti
Cast:	Ian Butcher, Andy Capie, Emma Cunniffe, Ben Daniels, Phil Davis, Gawn Grainger, David Hounslow, Richard Johnson, Nancy McLean, Lizzy McInnerny, Yvonne Riley, Ken Samuels, Sira Stampe, Glynne Steele
Awards:	2002 Laurence Olivier Award nomination: Best Lighting Designer (Howard Harrison)

A Lie of the Mind   28 June - 1 September 2001

Writer:	Sam Shepard
Director:	Wilson Milam
Designer:	Tom Piper
Lighting:	Tim Mitchell
Music Arrangements:	Andrew Ranken
Sound:	Fergus O'Hare
Cast:	Keith Bartlett, Anna Calder-Marshall, Sinéad Cusack, Catherine McCormack, Peter McDonald, Andy Serkis, Andrew Tiernan, Nicola Walker

Divas at the Donmar   3 - 29 September 2001

Designer:	Peter McKintosh
Lighting:	Stuart Crane
Sound:	Andy Brown

Clive Rowe

Musical Director:	Wendy Gadian
Musical Arrangements:	Neil McArthur

Siân Phillips

Director:	Thierry Harcourt
Musical Director and arrangements:	Kevin Amos

Michael Ball

Director:	Jonathan Butterell
Musical Director:	Jason Carr

The Little Foxes   4 October - 24 November 2001

Writer:	Lillian Hellman
Director:	Marianne Elliott
Designer:	Lez Brotherston
Lighting:	Paule Constable
Music:	Colin Towns
Sound:	John A Leonard
Cast:	Brid Brennan, David Calder, Christian Dixon, Peter Guinness, Michael Hadley, Edward Hughes, Matthew Marsh, Anna Maxwell Martin, Alibe Parsons, Penelope Wilton
Awards:	2001 Evening Standard Award nomination: Best Actress (Penelope Wilton)
	2002 Laurence Olivier Award nomination: Best Actress in a Supporting Role (Brid Brennan)
	2002 Laurence Olivier Award nomination: Best Set Designer (Lez Brotherston)

Privates On Parade   30 November 2001 - 2 March 2002

Writer:	Peter Nichols
Music and Lyrics:	Denis King
Director:	Michael Grandage
Designer:	Christopher Oram
Lighting:	Howard Harrison
Choreography:	Scarlett Mackmin
Musical Director:	Chris Walker
Sound:	Fergus O'Hare
Cast:	Roger Allam, Nigel Harman, David Hounslow, Wai-Keat Lau, James McAvoy, Hugh Sachs, Justin Salinger, Malcolm Sinclair, Daniel Tuite, Indira Varma, Carl Wu
Awards:	2002 Laurence Olivier Award: Best Actor (Roger Allam)
	2002 Laurence Olivier Award nomination: Best Actor in a Supporting Role (Malcolm Sinclair)
	2002 Laurence Olivier Award nomination: Best Theatre Choreographer (Scarlett Mackmin)

American Imports: 6 March - 13 June 2002

Jesus Hopped the 'A' Train   6 - 30 March

A LAByrinth Theater Company production, in association with Ron Kastner, Old Vic Productions plc and John Gould Rubin

London Premiere

Writer:	Stephen Adly Guirgis
Director:	Philip Seymour Hoffman
Designer:	Narelle Sissons
Costumes:	Mimi O'Donnell
Lighting:	Sarah Sidman
Sound:	Eric DeArmon
Cast:	Elizabeth Canavan, Salvatore Inzerillo, Ron Cephas Jones, John Ortiz, David Zayas

Frame 312
World Premiere

Writer:	Keith Reddin
Director:	Josie Rourke
Designer:	Tom Piper
Lighting:	David Plater
Sound:	Matt McKenzie
Cast:	Matt Bardock, Nicky Henson, Margot Leicester, Rachel Leskovac, Katherine Parkinson, Doraly Rosen

Lobby Hero
British Premiere

Writer:	Kenneth Lonergan
Director:	Mark Brokaw
Designer:	Robert Jones
Lighting:	Rick Fisher
Sound:	Fergus O'Hare
Cast:	Gary McDonald, Charlotte Randle, Dominic Rowan, David Tennant

Transferred to the New Ambassadors Theatre June - August 2002

Proof
British Premiere

Writer:	David Auburn
Director:	John Madden
Designer:	Rob Howell
Lighting:	Paule Constable
Composer:	Stephen Warbeck
Sound:	Tom Voegeli
Cast:	Richard Coyle, Gwyneth Paltrow, Ronald Pickup, Sara Stewart

Take Me Out   20 June - 3 August

A co-production with the Public Theater, NYC

World Premiere

Writer:	Richard Greenberg
Director:	Joe Mantello
Designer:	Scott Pask
Costumes:	Jess Goldstein
Lighting:	Kevin Adams
Sound:	Janet Kalas
Cast:	Kevin Carroll, Dominic Fumusa, Gene Gabriel, Neal Huff, Robert Jiménez, Joe Lisi, Denis O'Hare, Kohl Sudduth, Daniel Sunjata, Frederick Weller, James Yaegashi

Transferred to the Public Theater, New York August 2002

Divas at the Donmar   5 - 31 August 2002

Designer:	Dominic Fraser
Lighting:	Stuart Crane
Sound:	Andy Brown

Janie Dee

Musical Director:	Gareth Valentine

Ruby Turner

Philip Quast

Director:	Matthew Ryan
Musical Supervisor:	David White
Musical Director and Arranger:	Jason Robert Brown

Kristin Chenoweth

Musical Director:	Andrew Lippa

Uncle Vanya

6 September - 20 November 2002

Writers:	Brian Friel
	A version of the play by Anton Chekhov
Director:	Sam Mendes
Set Designer:	Anthony Ward
Costume Designer:	Mark Thompson
Lighting:	Hugh Vanstone
Music:	George Stiles
Sound:	Paul Arditti
Cast:	David Bradley, Selina Cadell, Luke Jardine, Helen McCrory, Cherry Morris, Anthony O'Donnell, Simon Russell Beale, Gyuri Sárossy, Mark Strong, Emily Watson

Twelfth Night

11 October - 30 November 2002

Writer:	William Shakespeare
Director:	Sam Mendes
Set Designer:	Anthony Ward
Costume Designer:	Mark Thompson
Lighting:	Hugh Vanstone
Music:	George Stiles
Sound:	Paul Arditti
Cast:	David Bradley, Selina Cadell, Luke Jardine, Paul Jesson, Helen McCrory, Cherry Morris, Anthony O'Donnell, Gary Powell, Simon Russell Beale, Gyuri Sárossy, Mark Strong, Emily Watson

WAREHOUSE PRODUCTIONS

Produced in association with Associated Capital Theatres Limited, The Shubert Organization and April Productions Limited.

The Real Inspector Hound/Black Comedy

Writers:	Tom Stoppard (The Real Inspector Hound)
	Peter Shaffer (Black Comedy)
Director:	Greg Doran
Designer:	Robert Jones
Lighting:	Howard Harrison
Sound:	John A Leonard

Yvonne Arnaud Theatre, Guildford 25 March - 4 April 1998

Richmond Theatre, Richmond 6 - 11 April 1998

Comedy Theatre, London 16 April - 31 October 1998

Cast: 25 March - 8 August 1998

Desmond Barrit, Anna Chancellor, Sara Crowe, Geoffrey Freshwater, Nichola McAuliffe, Joseph Millson (from 13 July), Nicholas Rowe (until 11 July), David Tennant, Gary Waldhorn

Cast: 10 August - 31 October 1998

David Bamber, Raymond Coulthard, Rachel Fielding, Geoffrey Freshwater, Amanda Harris, Nichola McAuliffe, Gary Powell, Neil Stacy

18 August - 23 October 1999

Director on tour:	David Grindley
Cast:	Jean Boht, Simon Chadwick, Sara Crowe, Robert Gill, Ian Hughes, Peter Cadden, Suzanna Klemm, Fred Perry, Vicky Seabrook, Neil Stacy, Barry Stanton, Sonya Walger

The Oxford Playhouse 18 - 28 August 1999

The Arts Theatre, Cambridge 31 August - 4 September 1999

The New Theatre, Hull 6 - 11 September 1999

Alhambra Theatre, Bradford 14 - 18 September 1999

Malvern Festival Theatre 20 - 25 September 1999

Theatre Royal, Bath 27 September - 2 October 1999

New Victoria Theatre, Woking 5 - 9 October 1999

Kings Theatre, Edinburgh 11 - 16 October 1999

Milton Keynes Theatre 19 - 23 October 1999

Suddenly Last Summer

Writer:	Tennessee Williams
Director:	Sean Mathias
Designer:	Tim Hatley
Lighting:	Mark Henderson
Original Music:	Jason Carr
Sound:	Aura Sound Design Ltd
Cast:	Patricia Boyer, Gerard Butler, Matt Fox, Sheila Gish, Johanna Kirby, Tim Matthews, Katherine Stark, Julia Swift, Sophie Turner, Rachel Weisz

Yvonne Arnaud Theatre, Guildford 3 - 13 March 1999
Theatre Royal, Bath 22 - 27 March 1999
Malvern Festival Theatre 29 March - 3 April 1999
Comedy Theatre, London 8 April - 17 July 1999

Awards: 2000 Laurence Olivier Award:
Best Lighting Designer (Mark Henderson)

Antigone

Writer:	Sophocles in a new version by Declan Donnellan
Director:	Declan Donnellan
Designer:	Nick Ormerod
Lighting:	Judith Greenwood
Music:	Paddy Cunneen
Movement:	Jane Gibson
Sound:	Aura Sound Design Ltd
Cast:	Kate Bowes, Christian Bradley, Anna Calder-Marshall, Finn Caldwell, Ryan Ellsworth, Tara Fitzgerald, Scott Frazer, Marshall Griffin, Jonathan Hyde, Damian Kearney, Owen McDonnell, Drew Mulligan, Donald Pirie, Richard Stacey, Anthony Taylor, Zubin Varla, Will Welch

Yvonne Arnaud Theatre, Guildford 6 - 18 September 1999
The Oxford Playhouse 20 - 25 September 1999
Old Vic, London 27 September - 18 December 1999

index

SAM MENDES

Dearest Caro,

I could write a book...

And to think that it was all because your desk faced the door, in the Barbican...

With thanks + love for your patience, loyalty, skill, forethought, stubbornness, cunning, friendship, judgement, taste, temper, face, hair + shoes.

S x

Many thanks to the following photographers:

Charlie Carter	33, 35 (bottom)
Andrew Crowley	96
Mark Douet	Contents page, 9 (top & left) 12,18,23,39 (top), 50, 56, 59, 76, 79, 81, 94, 99, 115, 118, 127, 129, 137 (top)
Jill Furmanovsky	140
Manuel Harlan	66, 135, 137 (bottom), 143
John Haynes	9 (bottom right), 62 (bottom), 122
Justine Jewkes	10, 14, 27, 129
Tristram Kenton	62 (top)
Ivan Kyncl	28, 35 (top), 39 (bottom), 49, 63, 71, 87, 89, 90, 93, 95, 131, 139
Michael Le Poer Trench	11, 21, 36, 42, 47, 53
Richard Mildenhall	65
Anne McNulty	15
Joan Marcus	43
Gordon Rainsford	4
Helen Ryan	14
Lorey Sebastian	128